NATIONAL SECUR

IMPLEMENTATION
OF THE DOD DIVERSITY AND
INCLUSION STRATEGIC PLAN

A FRAMEWORK FOR CHANGE THROUGH
ACCOUNTABILITY

NELSON LIM | ABIGAIL HADDAD | LINDSAY DAUGHERTY

Prepared for the Office of the Secretary of Defense

The research described in this report was sponsored by the Office of Personnel and Readiness in the Office of the Secretary of Defense (OSD) and conducted within the Forces and Resrouces Policy Center of the RAND National Defense Research Institute, a federally funded research and development center sponsored by OSD, the Joint Staff, the Unified Combatant Commands, the Navy, the Marine Corps, the defense agencies, and the defense Intelligence Community under Contract W74V8H-06-0002.

Library of Congress Cataloging-in-Publication Data

ISBN: 978-0-8330-8264-0

The RAND Corporation is a nonprofit institution that helps improve policy and decisionmaking through research and analysis. RAND's publications do not necessarily reflect the opinions of its research clients and sponsors.

Support RAND—make a tax-deductible charitable contribution at www.rand.org/giving/contribute.html

RAND® is a registered trademark

Cover design by Pete Soriano

© Copyright 2013 RAND Corporation

RAND OFFICES
SANTA MONICA, CA • WASHINGTON, DC
PITTSBURGH, PA • NEW ORLEANS, LA • JACKSON, MS • BOSTON, MA
DOHA, QA • CAMBRIDGE, UK • BRUSSELS, BE
www.rand.org

Preface

The Department of Defense (DoD) published its Diversity and Inclusion Strategic Plan in 2012. This report aims to discuss issues that DoD needs to consider in its implementation of the strategic plan and to provide a framework that DoD can use to organize its strategic initiatives. The framework categorizes the strategic initiatives specified in the DoD Diversity and Inclusion Strategic Plan along three key dimensions—compliance, communication, and coordination ("the three Cs")—and prioritizes them across time—short, medium, and long term. The framework can help all DoD components work toward the vision described in the strategic plan in a deliberate, synchronized effort by complying with current laws, regulations, and directives; communicating effectively to internal as well as external stakeholders; and coordinating efforts to ensure continuing change.

This work is intended to supplement the final report of the Military Leadership Diversity Commission (MLDC), *From Representation to Inclusion: Diversity Leadership for the 21st-Century Military*. The primary author of this RAND report was the research director of the MLDC effort, yet this report does not necessarily reflect the opinions of the MLDC commissioners. This work also draws from earlier RAND work, *Planning for Diversity: Options and Recommendations for DoD Leaders*, by Nelson Lim, Michelle Cho and Kimberly Curry Hall (Santa Monica, Calif.: RAND Corporation, MG-743-OSD, 2008); current organizational management literature; DoD strategic documents; and discussions with senior staff of the DoD Office of Diversity Management and Equal Opportunity (ODMEO).

The research was sponsored by the Office of Personnel and Readiness in the Office of the Secretary of Defense and conducted within the Forces and Resources Policy Center of the RAND National Defense Research Institute, a federally funded research and development center sponsored by the Office of the Secretary of Defense, the Joint Staff, the Unified Combatant Commands, the Navy, the Marine Corps, the defense agencies, and the defense Intelligence Community. For more information on the RAND Forces and Resources Policy Center, see http://www.rand.org/nsrd/ndri/centers/frp.html or contact the director (contact information is provided on the web page).

Contents

Figures

Tables

Summary

Two recent policy documents lay out a new vision for diversity in the U.S. Department of Defense (DoD): the Military Leadership Diversity Commission's (MLDC's) *From Representation to Inclusion: Diversity Leadership for the 21st Century Military* and the *Department of Defense Diversity and Inclusion Strategic Plan, 2012–2017*. These documents define the mission, set goals for diversity, and provide a general strategic framework for achieving these goals.

DoD has adopted a new definition of diversity:

> All the different characteristics and attributes of the DoD's Total Force, which are consistent with our core values, integral to overall readiness and mission accomplishment, and reflective of the nation we serve.

With this expansive definition, the *Department of Defense Diversity and Inclusion Strategic Plan, 2012–2017* contains three broad goals: (1) ensure leadership commitment to an accountable and sustained diversity effort; (2) employ an aligned strategic outreach effort to identify, attract, and recruit from a broad talent pool reflective of the best of the nation we serve; and (3) develop, mentor, and retain top talent from across the Total Force. Each of these broad goals is then broken into several narrower objectives, which in turn consist of one or more strategic actions and initiatives for accomplishing them. While the overall definition and goals are broad, the actions and initiatives are extremely specific. However, the document currently lacks structure: It does not suggest a prioritization among the actions/initiatives, objectives, or a timeline for accomplishing them. We suggest that to effectively imple-

xiii

ment these strategic objectives, DoD should approach the initiatives by classifying them according to which of three issues they address:

- DoD needs to clarify the relationship between equal opportunity (EO) compliance activities and diversity efforts.
- DoD needs to develop and implement communication strategies for its diversity vision for internal and external stakeholders.
- DoD needs to establish formal coordination among organizations that are responsible for various aspects of personnel policies and practices to sustain the momentum required for lasting diversity efforts to achieve the mission.

For each of these issues, we frame the stages of implementation into three major phases: short-term, medium-term, and long-term actions. The short term corresponds to the next 1–12 months, the mid term (1–3 years), and long term (4+ years). In addition, DoD will need to prioritize initiatives that can be implemented quickly and lay the groundwork for longer-term initiatives. In this austere fiscal environment, the prioritization of initiatives and coordination among stakeholders are essential elements for successful implementation of the strategic plan.

The purpose of this report is to provide a framework to support DoD in the implementation of its strategic plan, and to ensure that the resources devoted toward these efforts are targeted for long-term success. We argue that an enduring accountability system will be central to driving the significant changes across DoD that are needed to move toward the new vision for diversity. This accountability system will both anchor the goals by holding employees responsible for helping to meet them and allow DoD to measure progress and refine its processes on the basis of these outcomes. We also recommend communicating to employees how these goals fit in with DoD's mission and culture. We conducted a review of the general management, diversity management, and change management literature to build the framework for change through accountability. We supplemented our literature review with extensive policy discussions with the leadership of DoD's Office of Diversity Management and Equal Opportunity (ODMEO).

While we did review literature on this topic, it is difficult to fully ground recommendations in empirical evidence. Literature in this area tends to be highly theoretical, and even studies that attempt to measure the effects of certain types of policies or actions can rarely conduct the sort of experiments that are ideal for establishing the causal effects of policies or actions. Instead, researchers tend to perform case studies on organizations, or show correlations between policies or actions and outcomes. Because of this, while our recommendations are grounded in the appropriate literature, they are most properly viewed as hypotheses: We believe that these will help DoD reach its goals in this area, but we stress the importance of creating specific goals and tracking progress toward them.

Additionally, this study does not provide analysis of the suitability of DoD's diversity vision and its accompanying goals. DoD has already outlined its vision and goals; here we provide recommendations for how to better meet them. In addition, while we provide a high-level framework for the creation of an accountability system, we do not speak directly to how policies should be implemented. Given the current fiscal and organizational environment, DoD is undergoing often-drastic structural changes. Any attempt by us to fully describe how various organizations will execute different initiatives will quickly become obsolete, since the organizations themselves are changing as we write this report.

A Framework for Change Through Accountability

Accountability brings responsibility, and leaders who are made accountable and hold others accountable for supporting the vision for an organization will help to ensure that stakeholders move toward goals for accomplishing that vision (Babcock, 2009). We argue that the accountability system must be enduring, as DoD is a large organization characterized by constant change and frequent turnover in leadership. The system must be designed to cover the Total Force—i.e., both the military (active, reserve, and guard members) and civilian workforces—and be able to sustain personnel changes and shifts in leadership focus.

The DoD Diversity and Inclusion Strategic Plan emphasizes this as well, suggesting both the creation of a senior oversight body and the creation and monitoring of key diversity metrics. The framework for change through accountability is built on *compliance, communication,* and *coordination*—the three Cs—as shown in Figure S.1.

Pillar One: Compliance

The first pillar of the framework is *compliance.* If there are no clear and enforced rules about who is responsible for upholding diversity and inclusion-related policies and procedures, or for tracking metrics and meeting interim goals, then we believe it is unlikely that DoD will make significant progress toward its long-term goals for diversity and inclusion. Additionally, DoD must be compliant with two distinct, but related, aspects of diversity. The legal obligation to provide equal opportunity to protected groups and DoD policies on EO remain

Figure S.1
Framework for Change Through Accountability: The Three Cs

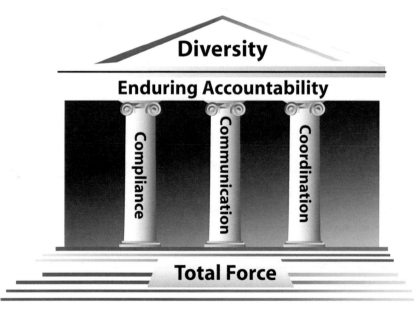

intact, and DoD must continue to protect these groups and monitor progress in demographic diversity. In particular, DoD must ensure that EO reporting requirements are being met, as there have been incomplete efforts to assure reporting of compliance in recent years. By standardizing EO metrics and reporting requirements, DoD can increase the transparency and consistency of this aspect of the accountability system for diversity. However, EO compliance is just one small part of the overall accountability system we propose. Diversity as it is more broadly defined by DoD requires an expanded set of compliance efforts to ensure that DoD is moving toward its newly defined goals of harnessing diversity to ensure mission effectiveness by creating an inclusive climate that allows all participants to reach their maximum potential.

As suggested by the old adage of "What gets measured gets done," metrics play a central role in compliance and are critical to accountability. As DoD moves to a broader view of diversity and an expanded set of goals centered on mission effectiveness, the metrics used to track compliance must be reconsidered and strategically refined to ensure alignment with these new goals. In recognition of this, the National Defense Authorization Act for Fiscal Year 2013, in a section titled "Diversity in the Armed Forces and Related Reporting Requirements," mandates that over the course of FY 2013, a "standard set of metrics and collection procedures that are uniform across the armed forces" shall be developed. DoD tracks a range of metrics related to demographic differences and collects data on workplace climate, but additional metrics, ones related to inclusion and that identify organizational barriers to diversity, are likely to be useful. Currently, DoD surveys service members regarding sexual harassment and sexual assault; the services may want to perform climate assessments related to other issues as well. The diversity metrics cover the employment life cycle of service members and civilian employees, including pre-accession outreach activities, accessions, assignments, educational opportunities, selections, and retention. By adopting a broad set of metrics aligned with diversity goals and standardized across the entire workforce, DoD can provide the foundation needed for a strong accountability system that will drive change.

Drawing on this conceptualization, we propose a prioritization scheme for compliance-related initiatives in Figure S.2. In the near term, or the next year, we recommend that DoD come into compliance with current Equal Employment Opportunity Commission (EEOC) requirements and evaluate existing internal requirements. Using the results of this evaluation and with an eye toward the eventual standardization of metrics across services and the combining of EO and military equal opportunity (MEO) structures—the structures within DoD that exist to ensure DoD compliance with internal EO requirements and external EEOC requirements—we also recommend that in the near term DoD create new internal metrics and procedures for evaluating compliance with EO requirements. In the medium term, or one to three years from now, we recommend that DoD issue and implement these new requirements. In the long term, or 4+ years from now, we recommend that DoD comply with these requirements.

Figure S.2
Recommended Steps and Timeline for Compliance Initiatives

1.

Ensure 100% Compliance with All EO Directives, Requirements, and Laws

Near Term
Meet all EEOC requirements
Evaluate and modify internal requirements

Medium Term
Issue and implement modified EO requirements
Combine MEO and EEO structures

Long Term
Comply with new Total Force EO requirements

RAND *RR333-S.2*

Pillar Two: Communication

Communication should explain the changes being made and convey both the importance of compliance to the organization and the consequences if compliance does not occur. It is also an opportunity to anchor the changes within the language and organizational values of the organization. Communication intended to drive movement toward a goal is often referred to as "strategic communication," which plays an important role in bridging the gap between organizations "knowing what they should do" and what is actually put into action (Pfeffer and Sutton, 2000). Too often, leaders in the midst of organizational change make the mistake of not communicating in the correct way, or not communicating enough (Riche et al., 2005). On the other hand, communication must not be seen as a substitute for action; communication should be designed to inspire action.

To ensure success in driving and managing change, strategic communication on diversity should be an active process, with DoD developing a plan around its goals, implementing the plan, evaluating the effectiveness of the communication strategies, and adjusting as necessary. In addition, communication that is driven by leadership and attentive to audiences will improve the likelihood of success in meeting DoD goals.

DoD faces a particular challenge in strategically communicating its new vision for diversity, because diversity efforts are typically seen as "head-counting exercises" focused exclusively on racial/ethnic and gender representations. One possibility for communicating the new vision for diversity as a concept distinct from EO policies is to integrate diversity leadership training into traditional leadership training, while retaining EO training as a separate effort. This integration reinforces the message that the ability to leverage differences for mission effectiveness is equal in importance and value to any other facet of leadership.

We also recommend, as suggested by organizational change literature, communicating how this plan fits into the organizational values of the services (National Defense Research Institute, 2010). The military is a meritocratic organization in which fairness is a major value. Training should stress both that discrimination is at odds with those values and that efforts to increase diversity and create an inclusive environment are intended to make sure that recruiting, training, hiring, and promotion processes are fully inclusive of potential talent, regardless of demographic or other factors, in an effort to make the services as high-performing and successful as possible. While communicating internally to the workforce is critical, communication strategies can also be used to reach external audiences, as these audiences play an essential role in DoD's ability to recruit a diverse workforce.

Drawing on this conceptualization, we propose a prioritization scheme for communication-related initiatives in Figure S.3. In the near term, or the next year, we recommend making some changes to existing training, both to consolidate current EO professional training and develop new diversity leadership training. We also recommend engaging in recruiting aimed at increasing personnel diversity. In the medium term, or from one to three years from now, we recommend implementing both diversity leadership and Total Force EO training as well as assessing the return on the near-term outreach efforts and

Figure S.3
Recommended Steps and Timeline for Communication Initiatives

Educate Current and Future Leaders, Reach Out to Communities

Near Term
Consolidate EO professional training
Develop diversity leadership training
Direct outreach activities to maximize efficiency
Develop clear diversity messages for external audiences

Medium Term
Implement Total Force EO professional training
Implement diversity leadership training
Evaluate return on investment from outreach efforts

Long Term
Develop and implement diversity leadership
    training for all members
Maintain robust outreach efforts

RAND *RR333-S.3*

modifying them if necessary. In the long term, or 4+ years from now, DoD should continue its outreach efforts and expand diversity leadership training to the Total Force, including service members in enlisted and officer training courses, such as the service academies.

Pillar Three: Coordination

To ensure that the accountability system achieves a consistent vision for diversity across DoD's large and diverse workforce, *coordination* is necessary. Coordination among stakeholders can also improve efficiency and reduce cost. Large organizational efforts can be hindered by complicated processes, overlap in efforts, and delays driven by differences in implementation. Enhanced coordination of effort can help further the new DoD diversity vision and its corresponding goals by appropriately allotting resources; assuring that all strategy-driven, planned efforts are in agreement; and developing operationally focused recruiting/hiring, training, development, and promotion efforts that work toward one vision.

Since 2006, ODMEO, under the Office of the Secretary of Defense (OSD), has been responsible for promoting EO and overseeing diversity policy for DoD (MLDC, 2011f, p. 96). ODEMO has organized the Defense Diversity Working Group (DDWG) to help the services synchronize efforts (MLDC, 2009b). We contend that the synchronization of efforts should be expanded and formalized. One possible way to formalize the coordination among key stakeholders is to establish the Defense Diversity Management System (DDMS) depicted in Figure S.4.

Coordination needs to happen not just among organizations that are responsible for diversity policies and practices; it must also include other "special-issue" organizations (which we refer to as "hot spots") that currently are considered to be outside the DoD diversity organizations. For instance, DoD Sexual Assault Prevention and Response is the organization responsible for the oversight of DoD sexual assault policy, including tracking data on sexual assault. DoD may also want to track other indicators that are also more indirectly related to inclusiveness of environment rather than overall diversity numbers. For instance, in the 1980s, black service members were overrepresented among court-

Figure S.4
An Example of a Formal Coordination Structure: The Defense Diversity
Management System

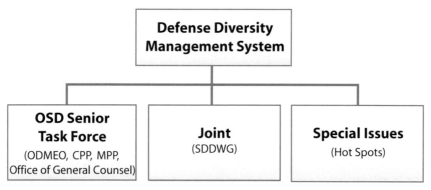

Potential Coordination Structure for Defense Diversity Management System

RAND *RR333-S.4*

martial convictions (Walker, 1992). It is not clear whether this is still the case, but this could be the sort of metric that DoD would look at as it goes beyond a focus on diversity numbers and looks at the broader environment. Moreover, coordination must also occur among ODMEO and other personnel organizations, such as Military Personnel Policy (MPP) and Civilian Personnel Policy (CPP), as well as the Office of General Council. The diversity organizations alone cannot improve diversity and create a climate of inclusion throughout DoD. For one thing, the diversity organizations have fewer resources than larger personnel organizations. More importantly, all personnel policies and practices—including outreach, recruiting, training, assignments, promotion, and retention—must be aligned with the overarching goal of promoting greater diversity and creating a more inclusive work environment. Support from the Office of General Counsel is imperative for a successful implementation of diversity efforts, as such efforts often involve interpretation of the law in dealing with protected groups in personnel policies. Without effective coordination, alignment among key stakeholders will not happen.

We suggest several areas in which coordination could be enhanced to support diversity efforts in additional ways, including increased leadership support, a specific leadership position for diversity, streamlined data management, and a process to coordinate focus on key diversity issues.

Based on this conceptualization, we propose a prioritization scheme—the DoD Diversity Management System (DDMS)—for coordination related initiatives in Figure S.5. In the near term, or the next year, DoD should organize several efforts: a senior OSD taskforce with representatives from various DoD agencies involved in personnel policy, the DDWG, and groups organized around specific issues (or "hot spots"), such as sexual assault, that hinder diversity. In the medium term, or one to three years from now, DoD should focus on creating the DDMS or a similar structure to oversee and coordinate

Figure S.5
Recommended Steps and Timeline for Coordination Initiatives

Coordinate Diversity Management Efforts for Maximum Efficiency

Near Term
Organize senior OSD task force
    (ODMEO, MPP, CPP, Office of General Counsel)
Organize joint senior-only DDWG
Organize special-issue organizations

Medium Term
Create centralized diversity management
    system (DDMS)

Long Term
Sustain centralized DDMS

RAND *RR333-S.5*

the three groups organized in the near-term step. In the long term, of 4+ years in the future, DoD should continue to sustain these efforts.

Recommendations

We provide DoD leadership with two recommendations:

Recommendation 1: Develop the accountability structure for diversity and inclusion based on the framework we proposed.

The framework we proposed is consistent with the *Department of Defense Diversity and Inclusion Strategic Plan, 2012–2017*. Table S.1 displays how the three Cs can be mapped onto DoD diversity strategic goals, objectives, actions, and initiatives, specified in the strategic plan.

It is important to communicate to employees that these initiatives, and the larger focus on diversity and inclusion, are a permanent change and not a function of the current political leadership (Terriff, 2007). Many government accountability programs are created "after the fact" of unsatisfactory efforts to reach goals or address problems (Curristine, 2005; Camm and Stecher, 2010); we recommend that DoD begin earlier, to avoid negative outcomes, rather than later, in response to them. We recommend that initial efforts related to each of the three Cs begin

Table S.1
The Three Cs Correlate with DoD Strategic Goals, Objectives, Actions, and Initiatives

Three Pillars	DoD Diversity Strategic Goals	Metrics
Comply	Action 1.1.1	Action 1.1.2 (2nd, 3rd, 4th initiatives)
Communicate		
Internal (Educate)	Action 3.1.1, Action 3.3.1	
External (Awareness)	Objective 2.1, Objective 2.2, Action 1.2.1	
Coordinate	Action 1.1.2 (1st initiative)	

NOTE: Remaining strategic actions concentrate on force sustainment.

early enough to seed a culture of change through accountability across DoD. A workforce that has accountability ingrained within its culture is more likely to be committed to the diversity vision, no matter who is leading the organization at a given time. By staying focused on accountability, DoD will be able to readily assess its workforce diversity as needed, disclose its performance, and refine and improve the functioning of the system across all components of the organization.

Recommendation 2: Establish a clear timeline of implementation milestones and publish annual status of progress toward these milestones for greatest transparency and accountability for progress.

Accountability must start with DoD diversity organizations, including ODMEO for the timely implementation of the strategic initiatives. Establishing a clear timeline of implementation milestones will facilitate discussions about resources and responsibilities among the stakeholders whose coordination is essential for successful implementation of DoD's Diversity and Inclusion Strategic Plan.

ODMEO should publish a progress report to inform external and internal stakeholders. This annual publication can become an important impetus that sustains the DoD diversity accountability system.

Acknowledgments

The authors wish to thank Clarence Johnson, Principal Director, Office of Diversity Management and Equal Opportunity (ODMEO), and Colonel J.J. Campbell, Executive Director of the Military Leadership Diversity Commission, for their extensive input on this project. We also thanks senior staff of ODMEO for providing information and participating in discussions about Department of Defense diversity policies and practices. We also thank Anny Wong for her valuable comments on the earlier draft. Catherine Chao provided administrative support to the RAND research team, and we offer our thanks to her as well. Finally we thank our reviewers, Sarah Meadows and Harry Thie of RAND, for their comprehensive and thoughtful reviews and suggestions.

Abbreviations

CDO	chief diversity officer
CNRC	Chief for Navy Recruiting Command
CPP	Civilian Personnel Policy
DDMS	DoD Diversity Management System
DDWG	Defense Diversity Working Group
DEOC	Defense Equal Opportunity Council
DEOMI	Defense Equal Opportunity Management Institute
DOD	U.S. Department of Defense
DUSD	Office of the Deputy Under Secretary of Defense
EEO	equal employment opportunity
EEOC	U.S. Equal Employment Opportunity Commission
EO	equal opportunity
GAO	U.S. Government Accountability Office
MEO	military equal opportunity
MEONet	Navy Military Equal Opportunity Network
MLDC	Military Leadership Diversity Commission
MPP	Military Personnel Policy
ODMEO	Office of Diversity Management and Equal Opportunity
OPM	U.S. Office of Personnel Management
OSD	Office of the Secretary of Defense
ROTC	Reserve Officers Training Corps

SAPRO   Sexual Assault Prevention and Response Office
SDDWG   Senior Defense Diversity Working Group

CHAPTER ONE

Introduction

Planning to Implementation

The past decade has seen a significant number of presidential executive orders aimed to bring about greater workplace diversity across the U.S. federal government. These include *Hispanic Employment in the Federal Government* (Executive Order 13171, October 2000), *Increasing Federal Employment of Individuals with Disabilities* (Executive Order 13548, July 2010), and *Establishing a Coordinated Government-Wide Initiative to Promote Diversity and Inclusion in the Federal Workforce* (Executive Order 13583, August 2011).

Executive Order 13583 (2011) instructs the U.S. Department of Defense (DoD) to make changes in how the department recruits, hires, develops, promotes, and retains its personnel. The executive order also urges DoD leaders to make a concerted, organized effort to "create a culture that encourages collaboration, flexibility, and fairness to enable individuals to participate to their full potential."

To comply with Executive Order 13583, DoD issued the *Department of Defense Diversity and Inclusion Strategic Plan, 2012–2017* in 2012. The strategic plan contains the official definition of diversity, goals, objectives, actions, and initiatives.

The Diversity and Inclusion Strategic Plan defines diversity as:

> Diversity is all the different characteristics and attributes of the DoD's Total Force, which are consistent with our core values, integral to overall readiness and mission accomplishment, and reflective of the nation we serve.

The Total Force refers to both the military (active, reserve, and guard members) and civilian workforces.

The Military Leadership Diversity Commission (MLDC) drafted this definition of diversity for DoD. In the National Defense Authorization Act for Fiscal Year 2009, Congress asked the MLDC to "develop a uniform definition of diversity to be used throughout DoD congruent with the core values and vision of DoD for the future workforce" (Pub L. 110-417), as each of the services were operating under slightly different definitions. Since the release of the MLDC report, DoD adopted the definition with slight modifications.

Notably, this definition is more inclusive than ever before. Based on the definition, diversity includes traditional characteristics, such as ethnicity, race, religion, and gender, as well as other attributes that can affect readiness and mission accomplishment. Even though the MLDC and DoD do not explicitly identify these attributes, the services have identified specific attributes in their policy statements. For example, Air Force Policy Directive 36-70 states, "Air Force Diversity includes but is not limited to: personal life experiences, geographic background, socio-economic background, cultural knowledge, educational background, work background, language abilities, physical abilities, philosophical/spiritual perspectives, age, race, ethnicity and gender" (2010, p. 2). In addition, this definition explicitly refers to DoD's Total Force—which includes military members of all components (including reserve and guard members) as well as civilian employees.

DoD's definition of diversity reflects the consensus among diversity professionals that diversity must apply to everyone in the organization in order to achieve an inclusive work climate (Lim, Cho, and Curry, 2008). Similar definitions are utilized by such major corporations as Lockheed Martin, the Disney Interactive Media Group, and General Electric (MLDC, 2009a). These organizations define diversity in terms of a broad range of human differences and tend to assert that diversity can increase organizational effectiveness, performance, and innovation (Lockheed Martin, no date; Disney Interactive Media, no date; General Electric Company, no date; Thomas, 2005).

DoD's definition of diversity, however, poses several challenges to DoD in its implementation efforts. First, internal and external stakeholders—including minority and female civilian employees and service members, members of Congress, and civil society at large—may view the broad definition as DoD's attempt to step away from meeting the challenge of increasing the representation of minorities and women among senior leaders (Lim, Cho, and Curry, 2008, p. 18). Second, the new definition makes it difficult to track the performance of diversity initiatives and hold leaders accountable for progress. It is impossible to measure "all the different characteristics and attributes of DoD's Total Force." As Lim, Cho, and Curry (2008, p. 18) write, based on the new definition, "DoD has already achieved [structural] diversity according to this definition, for the Fourth Estate alone is made up of the Washington Headquarters Services and its 16 serviced components, as well as 14 distinct DoD Agencies."

In addition to providing definition of diversity, the DoD Diversity and Inclusion Strategic Plan contains three goals, eight objectives, 13 actions, and 37 initiatives (DoD, 2012a). Initiatives are nested under actions, which are nested under objectives, which in turn are nested under goals.

The DoD Diversity and Inclusion Strategic Plan's three goals are as follows:

1. Ensure leadership commitment to an accountable and sustained diversity effort
2. Employ an aligned strategic outreach effort to identify, attract, and recruit from a broad talent pool reflective of the national we serve
3. Develop, mentor, and retain top talent from across the Total Force.

These goals clearly demonstrate that increasing diversity and creating an inclusive work climate must involve organizations beyond DoD's diversity organizations. DoD's diversity organizations not only have fewer resources and lesser authority than organizations that manage military and civilian personnel; they also cannot directly bring about changes in personnel policies and practices. For example, DoD's Office of Diversity Management and Equal Opportunity (ODMEO) has fewer resources than Military Personnel Policy (MPP) and Civilian Personnel Policy (CPP). More importantly, MPP and CPP can establish and maintain personnel policies and practices, while ODMEO cannot.

To implement these strategic initiatives, DoD needs to address a variety of issues:

- Comply with U.S. laws and regulations as well as DoD's own directives and policies.
- Communicate its diversity vision to both internal and external stakeholders.
- Coordinate formally among organizations that are responsible for various aspects of personnel policies and practices to sustain momentum required for lasting diversity efforts to achieve the mission.

In addition, DoD will need to prioritize initiatives that can be implemented quickly and pave the groundwork for longer-term initiatives. In the current austere fiscal environment, the prioritization of initiatives and coordination among stakeholders are essential elements for successful implementation of the strategic plan.

Purpose of This Report

The purpose of this report is to provide a framework to support DoD's efforts to implement its Diversity and Inclusion Strategic Plan. DoD leadership has successfully developed a vision for a diverse, effective, and efficient workforce and has identified numerous initiatives that will be implemented to achieve this vision. The framework we present centers on what we call the three Cs: *compliance, communication*, and *coordination*. By following the proposed framework, DoD will be able to establish an enduring accountability system that will support the new vision for diversity through a deliberate, coordinated effort by *complying* with current law and new diversity policies, *communicating* the new vision in a strategic way, and *coordinating* efforts to ensure that the change is system-wide and enduring. We frame the stages of implementation into three major phases: short, medium, and long term.

Methodology

We rely on two recent documents as our primary sources to identify and understand DoD's vision, goals, and strategic plan for diversity: *From Representation to Inclusion: Diversity Leadership for the 21st Century Military* (MLDC, 2011f) and the *Department of Defense Diversity and Inclusion Strategic Plan, 2012–2017* (DoD, 2012a). To identify best practices for implementation, we conducted a literature review of general management, diversity management, and change management literature. We also drew from a prior RAND report on diversity in DoD, *Planning for Diversity: Options and Recommendations for DoD Leaders* (Lim, Cho, and Curry, 2008), as well as the implementation chapter from the RAND report *Sexual Orientation and U.S. Military Policy: An Update of RAND's 1993 Study* (National Defense Research Institute, 2010). Finally, we used information from policy discussions with key stakeholders in ODMEO as a source of additional insights.

Limitations of the Study

This study does not analyze the suitability of the new vision for diversity and its accompanying goals, as DoD has already determined its goals for diversity and has set forth a strategy for accomplishing them. In addition, while we provide a high-level framework for the creation of an accountability system, we do not speak directly to how policies should be implemented. Given the current fiscal and organizational environment, DoD is undergoing structural changes. Any attempt by us to fully describe how various organizations will execute different initiatives will quickly become obsolete, since the organizations themselves are changing.

In addition, while we draw from a large body of literature, there is a limited number of large-scale studies on effective management strategies for diversity, so many of the best practices found in the literature are theoretical or based on case studies of a limited number of organizations. In general, literature in this area tends to be highly theoretical, and even studies that attempt to measure the effects of certain types of policies or actions can rarely conduct the sort of experiments that are ideal for establishing the causal effects of policies or actions. DoD is also distinct from many of the organizations studied in management literature in the size and structure of its workforce and its organizational mission, so the findings from corporate experiences may not apply to DoD. Because of these issues, while our recommendations are grounded in the appropriate literature, they are most properly viewed as hypotheses: We believe that these will help DoD reach its goals in this area, but we stress the importance of creating specific goals and tracking progress toward them.

Organization of This Report

The next five chapters describe a framework to assist DoD in the implementation of the DoD Diversity and Inclusion Strategic Plan. In Chapter Two, we describe the framework as a whole. In Chapters Three through Five, we focus on the three Cs—*compliance, communication,* and *coordination*—that we argue are the three pillars providing the foundation for an effective accountability system. In the concluding chapter, we describe how elements of the framework correlate with the goals, objectives, and initiatives of the DoD Diversity and Inclusion Strategic Plan.

A Note on Terminology

This report refers to equal opportunity (EO), equal employment opportunity (EEO), military equal opportunity (MEO), and the Equal Employment Opportunity Commission (EEOC). EO refers to a set of principles regarding how people should be treated, including in an employment context. It can also refer to formal requirements relating to these principles, both the requirements that DoD has set for itself and those that have been set by or are enforced by the EEOC, a federal agency that makes and enforces EO-related rules. EEO and MEO refer to structures within DoD that exist to ensure compliance with these requirements for both the civilian and military workforces.

CHAPTER TWO

A Framework for Change Through Accountability

In this chapter, we introduce a framework that uses accountability to support change toward DoD's new vision of diversity. This framework will help DoD categorize and prioritize the 38 diversity strategic initiatives specified in the DoD Diversity and Inclusion Strategic Plan. The framework conceptualizes implementation tasks into three Cs— *compliance*, *communication*, and *coordination*—and stages the tasks into three major phases—short, medium, and long term.

The Role of Accountability in Diversity Efforts

To realize the vision and achieve the goals stated in the DoD Diversity and Inclusion Strategic Plan, DoD leaders must transform the ways they recruit, develop, promote, and retain their personnel.

All organizational transformations are difficult (Fernandez and Rainey, 2006). Policymaking can be slow, and new initiatives, such as those that support DoD's diversity vision, can take five to seven years to become routine in large public- and private-sector organizations (GAO, 2011). Organizational transformation will be especially difficult for DoD, for several reasons. DoD organizational structure is extremely complex. DoD leaders are rotated frequently, often having only three to four years to achieve their goals in a particular position. DoD is exceptional in its enormity; recognized as the largest employer in the world, DoD consists of 3.2 million personnel who serve as active duty service members, as well as guardsmen, reservists, and civilian support (Alexander, 2012).

Hence, the MLDC argues that the new vision for diversity will not be achieved and sustained unless there is "a system of accountability, monitoring, and enforcement to ensure continued progress" (2011f, p. 95). More importantly, the accountability system must be *enduring*, meaning that all DoD components and personnel will be able to act according to diversity standards and persist in these actions even if there are significant changes in leadership. Without such a system, there is a risk that fostering and managing diversity for mission effectiveness will be viewed merely as the concern of one or two leaders, and the diversity initiatives will not gain the momentum necessary for lasting organizational change.

An accountability system that is clearly based on the strategic vision and goals can make the priorities for change more salient. In addition, the existence of an effective accountability system fosters trust from internal and external stakeholders, as it demonstrates the commitment by the leaders to improve diversity and create an inclusive work environment for all personnel (Fernandez and Rainey, 2006).

In the next section, we present a framework for this accountability system as a means of achieving the new vision for diversity.

Diversity Efforts Must Encompass the Total Force

Any implementation framework for DoD diversity efforts must address the needs of the Total Force, which includes civilian and military personnel across all services and the Fourth Estate.[1] The MLDC's *From Representation to Inclusion* (2011f) focused on the changes that should occur in the military because the commission lacked the authority to make recommendations for the civilian force, but the commissioners emphasize, "This omission should not imply that the diversity of the civilian workforce is not important for DoD. On the contrary, a diverse civilian workforce is critical to the 21st century military because this group is an essential element of the Total Force." The DoD Diversity

---

[1] The Fourth Estate consists of the defense agencies, DoD field activities, and defense-wide programs.

and Inclusion Strategic Plan acknowledges the importance of including the Total Force in the new vision for diversity by drawing from both U.S. Office of Personnel Management (OPM) and MLDC recommendations. Given that diversity is now considered a means to mission effectiveness by DoD, and that both the civilian workforce and the military workforce are critical to mission effectiveness, efforts to improve mission effectiveness must include the Total Force.

A Framework for Change Through Accountability

The implementation framework we propose addressed the needs of the Total Force and is supported by an enduring accountability system, which is in turn built on the three pillars of *compliance, communication,* and *coordination*—which we refer to as three Cs.

Figure 2.1
Framework for Change Through Accountability: The Three Cs

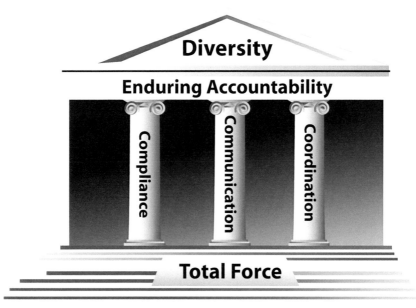

Pillar One: Compliance

The first pillar of our framework is *compliance*. Compliance is a key component of any accountability system. DoD must comply with U.S. laws and regulations as well as DoD's own directives and policies. If individuals and organizations are able to circumvent the policies and procedures required to achieve diversity and are not held accountable for tracking metrics and meeting interim goals, then the system lacks any true accountability, and it is unlikely that DoD will make significant progress toward its long-term goals for diversity. DoD must be compliant with two distinct, but related, aspects of diversity. First, the legal obligation to provide equal opportunity to protected groups and to comply with DoD policies on EO remains intact, and DoD must continue to focus on efforts to support these groups and provide evidence of progress in demographic diversity. In addition, the expanded vision for diversity requires a broader conception of inclusion and opportunity, with efforts to enhance diversity across a much larger set of characteristics.

Pillar Two: Communication

Communication is critical to supporting an accountability system, mainly to ensure that stakeholders understand the vision and goals they are being held accountable for and to help the organization move toward desired change by changing the culture and increasing the transparency of the system to enhance "buy-in." Communication intended to drive movement toward a goal is often referred to as "strategic communication." DoD defines strategic communication as the "orchestration and/or synchronization of actions, images, and words to achieve a desired effect" (Joint Publication 1-02, 2007). Strategic communication has come to the forefront of military leaders and thinkers in the past decade: Tactical commanders have routinely had to employ communication strategies in Iraq and Afghanistan during "deterrent operations" targeting potential adversaries' decisionmaking capabilities (Stavridis, 2007, p. 4).

Strategic communication plays an important role in bridging the gap between something that organizations "know they should do" and something that is actually put into action (Pfeffer and Sutton,

2000). Too often, leaders in the midst of organizational change make the mistake of not communicating in the correct way, or not communicating enough. In addition, research shows that people of different backgrounds may hear the same thing but understand it differently (Riche et al., 2005). Leaders may wrongly believe that others understand issues as complex as diversity and see the new vision as clearly as they do, so it is critical to take steps to ensure that this is actually the case. However, communication must not be seen as a substitute for action; communication should be designed to inspire action. This is the distinction between strategic communication and "communication for communication's sake."

Diversity communication efforts should proceed along two distinct tracks. First, DoD should communicate the new vision for diversity to internal audiences as a concept distinct from EO policies. This distinction can be articulated by integrating diversity leadership concepts into traditional leadership training, while retaining EO training as a separate effort. This integration will reinforce the message that the ability to leverage differences for mission effectiveness is equal in importance and value to any other facet of leadership. Second, while communication internally to the workforce is critical, communication strategies can also be used to reach external audiences, as these audiences play an essential role in DoD's ability to recruit and retain a diverse workforce.

Pillar Three: Coordination

By *coordination*, we refer to the synchronization of efforts by all of the military services and agencies of DoD to ensure a unity of effort. To ensure that the accountability system achieves a consistent vision for diversity across the large, diverse DoD workforce, coordination is necessary. Fragmented efforts can decrease the chance for success by complicating processes, resourcing similar efforts, and delaying the completion of decisionmaking or fulfilling tasks. Enhanced coordination of effort can help further the new DoD diversity vision and its corresponding goals by appropriately allotting resources; assuring that all strategy-driven, planned efforts are in agreement; and developing operationally focused recruiting/hiring, managing, and promotion efforts that work toward one vision.

Currently, DoD engages in a range of critical efforts aiming to optimize workforce diversity. However, the MLDC found that these efforts vary across the services, which operated with different definitions of diversity and thus often had goals and initiatives bringing different visions to fruition. DoD has begun consolidating its diversity efforts since the 2011 MLDC review. Executive Order 13583 (2011) asks that the organization work harder at consolidating diversity efforts:

> Wherever possible, the Federal Government must also seek to consolidate compliance efforts established through related or overlapping statutory mandates, directions from Executive Orders, and regulatory requirements. By this order, I am directing executive departments and agencies . . . to develop and implement a more comprehensive, integrated, and strategic focus on diversity and inclusion as a key component of their human resources strategies.

Further, the DoD Diversity and Inclusion Strategic Plan begins to show how both the civilian and military workforces can streamline efforts to work toward change.

However, the coordination must go beyond DoD diversity organizations. The coordination must occur among ODMEO and other personnel organizations, such as MPP and CPP, as well as the Office of General Council. The diversity organizations alone cannot improve diversity and create a climate of inclusion throughout DoD. For one thing, the diversity organizations have fewer resources than larger personnel organizations. More importantly, all personnel policies and practices, ranging from outreach, recruiting, training, assignments, promotion, to retention, must be aligned with the overarching goal of promoting greater diversity and creating a more inclusive work environment. Similarly, support from the Office of General Council is imperative for a successful implementation of diversity efforts, as such efforts often involve interpretation of the law in dealing with protected groups in personnel policies. Without effective coordination, the alignment among key stakeholders will not happen.

Moving Forward

In the next three chapters, we expand our description of compliance, communication, and coordination. We start each chapter by describing why the pillar plays an important role in supporting accountability and change in the area of diversity. We then highlight areas that require special attention as DoD develops and implements its diversity strategy. Finally, we provide a conclusion with some recommendations for how the framework can be used by DoD to structure and prioritize efforts for diversity.

CHAPTER THREE

Compliance

DoD efforts to improve diversity and inclusion are new, and there are few policy directives that govern these efforts. But there are well-established U.S. laws and regulations as well as DoD's directives and policies regarding equal employment opportunity (EEO) and military equal opportunity (MEO). These requirements are about providing equal opportunity for all personnel, regardless of their background. The major federal law regarding workplace discrimination is the Civil Rights Act of 1964, which prohibits discriminatory employment decisions or actions based on a person's race, color, religion, sex, or national origin (42 U.S.C. § 2000e-2). The U.S. Equal Employment Opportunity Commission (EEOC) is the federal law enforcement agency charged with enforcing workplace discrimination law, including the Civil Rights Act of 1964, federal regulations, and court decisions. The military component of DoD is granted some exceptions from EEOC rules: They are allowed to use age, disability, and gender in certain employment decisions. However, by and large, EEOC compliance within DoD is similar to EEOC compliance for other large employers, particularly large federal government employers.

The Importance of Compliance

Although DoD wishes to go beyond just compliance and pursue diversity and inclusion in deeper ways, it is still obligated to comply with external and internal rules regarding discrimination. The EEOC mandates that employers not discriminate on the basis of various attributes, create a workplace free from harassment based on those attributes, provide reasonable accommodations to workers based on religious beliefs and disability, and not retaliate against employees who make discrimination complaints or assist with investigations. In addition, there are various other requirements in service of these larger goals, including the amount of time that employers have to respond to employee EO complaints and benchmarking reports that must be performed and submitted. While evaluating the degree to which DoD is complying with EEOC requirement is beyond the scope of this report, we do have some evidence that compliance is incomplete (which we present later in this chapter).

Additionally, there are various requirements specific to DoD, some of which DoD is out of compliance with. For the most part, these compliance-related directives are better seen not as creating new requirements for nondiscrimination, but as signaling leadership commitment and creating processes designed to increase compliance with EEOC requirements. For instance, some directives require DoD to report on its own EO activities, or on aspects of employment, such as hiring and retention by demographic group. Some are symbolic, signaling leadership commitment to demographic diversity.

This chapter offers recommendations for how DoD can better comply with both internal and external directives. Not being in compliance with external rules is illegal, and not complying with internal directives both sends a negative signal about DoD's commitment to EO and diversity and reduces the chances of EEOC compliance. However, it is also possible that current internal EO directives are outdated or redundant, so we recommend evaluating them and making changes as needed. In addition to evaluating requirements and coming into compliance, we recommend combining EO and MEO into one function in order to reduce redundancies.

Federal Law Mandates Nondiscrimination and a Workplace Free from Harassment

Like all employers, DoD is obligated to meet a variety of EO requirements put forth by the federal government, although it has some discretion in terms of how it meets those requirements. Two bodies of law govern the use of race, ethnicity, color, national origin, gender, and religion in the context of employment by the government:

- The Equal Protection Clause of the Fourteenth Amendment: One of the Civil War–era amendments to the U.S. Constitution, courts have interpreted the brief statement in the Fourteenth Amendment to mean that government laws or programs that use different standards based on individuals' race, color, ethnicity, national origin, and religion (and, to a lesser extent, gender) unlawfully discriminate on the basis of membership in a suspect class.
- Title VII of the Civil Rights Act of 1964 (as amended): This body of law generally forbids discriminatory employment decisions or actions based on a person's race, color, religion, sex, or national origin (42 U.S.C. § 2000e-2).

The military is something of an exception among public employers because it has been granted unusual flexibility to select individuals based on age and disability and, to a very limited extent, gender, based on current military requirements. However, in general it is still prohibited from using different standards in admission, accession, assignment, promotion, or separation decisions based on an individual's race, color, ethnicity, gender, or religion.

The Role of Metrics in Compliance

Complying with external requirements goes beyond tracking demographic diversity numbers, although it does include that. This section describes the use of metrics in compliance and several different types of metrics that are useful in evaluating EO compliance.

Measuring outcomes is a major part of ensuring that an employer is in compliance with EO rules. Practitioners have found that tracking metrics and setting benchmarks help to overcome resistance to change, provide a structure for external evaluation, and, through their development, create new networks of communication among offices, departments, and personnel (Camp, 1995). By *metrics,* we refer to measures of key variables of interest and their measurement, and by *benchmarks,* we refer to targets against which to judge progress.

DoD uses a range of metrics to track demographic representation and collects data via climate surveys, but these requirements are changing in response to new legislation and new and broader diversity efforts. For instance, the National Defense Authorization Act for Fiscal Year 2013, in a section titled "Diversity in the Armed Forces and Related Reporting Requirements," mandates that over the course of FY 2013, a "standard set of metrics and collection procedures that are uniform across the armed forces" shall be developed. Specifically, the metrics must be designed:

> . . . to accurately capture the inclusion and capability aspects of the armed forces' broader diversity plans, including race, ethnic, and gender specific groups, as potential factors of force readiness. (Pub. L. 112-239, Section 519)

Best practices from the literature suggest that metrics should be *strategic,* in that they convey information about values and priorities (Babcock, 2009; Kraus and Riche, 2006; Holvino, Ferdman, and Merrill-Sands, 2004; Melnyk, Stewart, and Swink, 2004). The MLDC advised that such metrics reflect the following qualities:

- **Developed with the diversity vision in mind:** Metrics should link intended goals, strategies, and actual execution. Metrics not linked to a strategic end state do not create value for organizations (Boudreau and Ramstad, 1998).
- **Clearly stated:** Metrics should be easily understood and communicated.
- **Value added:** Metrics should deliver value to the organization by providing information on key aspects of performance.
- **Actionable to drive improvements:** Good metrics provide information that has implications for a clear plan of action.
- **Tracked over time:** Metrics must be tracked over time to provide information on the trend in the metric, not simply its status at one moment in time.

- **Verifiable:** Metrics should be based on an agreed upon set of data and a documented process for converting data into the measure. Given the same data and process, independent sources should arrive at the same metric value (MLDC, 2011e).

In the following sections, we briefly describe several categories of metrics for assessing diversity throughout the DoD workforce. The degree to which DoD currently uses these metrics and/or intends to expand them varies.

Metrics That Quantify Demographic Representation

The MLDC found that the most well-developed metrics to date were those aimed at characterizing the racial, ethnic, and gender diversity of the DoD workforce. The services track diversity according to these metrics at a range of points through the career pipeline, including recruitment, accessions, retention, and promotion. The demographic makeup of the workforce is typically benchmarked against the national population, the future national population, and the eligible population (MLDC, 2011e). Currently, the services' diversity tracking efforts are not coordinated, and each service's data and reporting systems have been developed to meet internal service needs, so their systems and metrics vary. We discuss the need for standardization across metrics later in this chapter.

Metrics That Describe Organizational Diversity Climates

"Organizational climate" refers to personnel's shared perception of policies, practices, and procedures in their workplace, and how certain behaviors are rewarded, expected, and supported.[1] Assessments of organizational climates are conducted when leaders need insight into employees' expectations and satisfaction levels, how they interpret their organization's culture, and how open they are to change (Scott et al., 2003). Research suggests that climate assessments may be important because personnel policy changes, especially those perceived to "seek to

---

[1] Adapted from Scheider, Ehrhart, and Macey, 2012; this definition is similar to that found in MLDC's *Decision Paper #8: Metrics* (MLDC, 2011e).

enhance the integration of identity groups," can elicit negative reactions if the climate of an organization is not managed properly (Kossek and Zonia, 1993, p. 62). A positive EO climate is associated with organizational commitment, job satisfaction, and a perception of workgroup effectiveness, whereas negative EO behaviors, such as racial and sexual discrimination, are associated with lower job satisfaction, lower commitment, and lower perceptions of workgroup effectiveness (Estrada, Stetz, and Harbke, 2007; McIntyre et al., 2002).

The military currently utilizes a number of surveys to assess EO aspects of climate (MLDC, 2011e).[2] No one climate survey can or should be expected to "do it all." A recent study on organizational climate assessment finds that to understand the full picture on any important issue in an organization, leaders need multiple *kinds* of assessments: "a plurality of conceptualizations, tools, and methods are more likely to offer robust, subtle, and useful insights" (Scott et al., 2003). Since MLDC, federal agencies have expressed the need to develop and/or refine climate assessments that are aligned with the broader definition of *diversity*. In November 2011, OPM released *Guidance for Agency-Specific Diversity and Inclusion Strategic Plans*. In addition to measures of diversity in the workforce, the guide emphasizes the need to track measures of inclusion, meaning "a culture that encourages collaboration, flexibility, and fairness to enable individuals to contribute to their full potential and further retention" (U.S. OPM, 2011, p. 23).

Metrics That Focus on Processes

The impact of new diversity efforts on the makeup of DoD's military workforce may take time to materialize, particularly given the fact that the personnel system within the military is a closed one: Most new service members enter either as junior enlisted personnel or junior officers, and there is limited lateral hiring to higher ranks. In addition, it may be difficult to measure some of the key outcomes of diversity efforts.

---

2   For example, the Armed Forces Workplace and Equal Opportunity (WEO) Surveys, the Armed Forces Workplace and Gender Relations (WGR) Surveys, and the Status of Forces Survey (SOFS), the Defense Equal Opportunity Management Institute (DEOMI) Organizational Climate Survey (DEOCS), and the DEOMI Diversity Management Climate Survey (DDMCS).

When outcome measures are difficult to obtain in the immediate term, there can be substantial value to tracking processes to ensure they are being carried out appropriately (Stecher et al., 2010). As a result, DoD may wish to develop metrics focusing on processes: for instance, the creation of certain types of diversity and EO-related infrastructure. However, as the movement toward the new vision of diversity matures, metrics should increasingly shift from processes to outcomes (Stecher et al., 2010).

Metrics That Locate Organizational Barriers

Identifying barriers that may be preventing DoD from meeting its goals for diversity is a necessity, and when there are significant disparities of certain types, barrier analysis is required by the EEOC. For example, structural barriers, such as the combat exclusion policy for women, have historically prevented women from serving in the tactical and operational career fields (such as infantry in the Army) that are helpful to becoming a top leader.[3] There are also perceptual barriers, wherein people of different racial and ethnic backgrounds perceive the actions of others differently. Perceptual barriers can manifest both as the beliefs of leadership that individuals with certain characteristics do not have equal capabilities, and as individuals' beliefs that discrimination is driving outcomes they see as unfair. There are ways to overcome both structural and perceptual barriers: Sweeping changes can be made, such as the re-examination of the "Don't Ask, Don't Tell" policy in 2011, and more "boots on the ground" approaches can be employed, such as mentoring programs and revitalized outreach efforts.

A barrier analysis is a methodical examination of the recruitment, hiring, and promotion processes in an agency to determine where women and minorities face obstacles that might account for their less-

---

[3]   DoD rescinded the direct combat exclusion policy on January 24, 2013, and is working on a plan for implementation and integration of women into closed positions. However, some positions may retain gender restrictions (U.S. Department of Defense, Office of the Assistant Secretary of Defense for Public Affairs, 2013). It is also unclear the degree to which an elimination of formal barriers will result in significant gender integration due both to different occupational preferences and gender-neutral physical standards that disqualify a higher proportion of female service members than male service members.

than-proportionate representation among applicants, hires, and upper management. A set of standardized metrics based on diversity benchmarks can help identify opportunities to improve programs and reinforce a culture of EO and diversity. EEOC Management Directive 715 (Equal Employment Opportunity Commission, 2003) offers strong and clear policy guidance for federal agencies to conduct a barrier analysis to identify and eliminate barriers that impede free and open competition in their workplaces. A recent RAND document identifies five phases to conducting a barrier analysis (Haddad et al., 2012):

- **Develop a detailed flow chart of the workforce management process.** The objective of this phase is to map out workforce management processes at key points in the career lifecycle in order to identify potential barriers to diversity.
- **Construct population benchmarks.** Establishing benchmarks is important to compare whether certain groups are under- or overrepresented at different points in the career lifecycle.
- **Compare employee distribution to benchmarks.** The objective of this phase is to determine whether there is a discrepancy between population benchmarks and the DoD workforce at various points in the career lifecycle.
- **Identify potential barriers.** Discrepancies found between benchmarks and the DoD population, administrative data, exploratory surveys, or interviews could be used to uncover barriers.
- **Address or remove barriers.** The objective in this final phase is to develop solutions to barriers found in Phase 4.

Standardizing Metrics for Accountability

The MLDC recommendations emphasize the need to develop a top-level set of common strategic metrics to support a sustainable diversity strategy. Recently, ODMEO has begun exploring the possibility of using Defense Manpower Data Center data to establish a baseline for the standardization of metrics. The services' diversity tracking efforts are not currently coordinated—each service's data and reporting systems are developed to meet its own internal needs—so their systems and metrics vary. For the purposes of the MLDC's research effort, a particularly troublesome area of inconsistency was in how the services analyze and present data by race and ethnicity. For example, some services reported race and ethnicity separately, while other services created mutually exclusive race and ethnicity groups. These inconsistencies existed despite the fact that there is explicit guidance from the White House Office of Management and Budget on how federal agencies should collect and report such data.

Beyond standardizing EO reporting, the MLDC calls for standardized metrics across all dimensions of diversity, which can help leaders identify opportunities to improve programs and reinforce a culture of EO and diversity throughout the DoD workforce. Metrics and evaluations can help assure compliance and accountability in that results indicate how well a policy or program vision is realized; assessments provide leaders with evidence of how well the organization is performing in the ways they intend.

Noncompliance with Internal Requirements

We provide evidence of several gaps in compliance with internal policies and directives below. This by no means is a comprehensive list; only a full study on the "state of reporting" throughout DoD could elicit such results. These gaps suggest that greater attention needs to be given to reporting and metrics for DoD to fully comply with the law and foster a lasting diversity effort.

- **The Human Goals Charter:** Department of Defense Directive 1440.1 (1987, p. 4) mandated that DoD "prepare a new DoD Human Goals Charter each time a new Secretary of Defense is appointed." The MLDC (2011f, p. 29) assessed the importance of this charter as it helps to strengthen diversity as a core value and "inculcate it into each of [the Services'] cultures throughout the servicemember life cycle." In his presentation at the March 2010 MLDC meeting, Claiborne Haughton, former Acting Deputy Assistant Secretary of Defense for EO, described the process for charter renewal and the clear signal it sends as to the vision for diversity (MLDC, 2011f). However, the last charter was signed in 1998, by then–Secretary of Defense William Cohen.

- **MEO reporting:** Department of Defense Directive 1350.2 (1995), which gives guidance particular for military EO cases, requires each DoD component to submit an annual MEO assessment that reports on, among other things, demographic differences in promotions, retention, and assignments. This is the sole reporting mechanism required by DoD on affirmative action and EO policies for military personnel. Compliance with this part of the directive has been lacking, however; the last MEO assessment report was produced in 2004, using FY 2002 data (MLDC, 2010a).
- **Defense Equal Opportunity Council (DEOC) reporting:** Established in 1987, the DEOC was given the responsibility to "advise the Secretary of Defense on policies for EO matters, coordinate policy and review the military and civilian EO programs, monitor progress of program elements, assist in developing policy guidance for education and training in EO and human relations for DoD personnel, and provide oversight and ensure resources for the Defense Equal Opportunity Management Institute (DEOMI)" (Department of Defense Directive 1350.2, 1995). DEOC members presented regular progress reports on how well DoD was meeting EO goals and appointed members to attend to specific issues by forming working committees, such as the DEOC Task Force on Discrimination and Sexual Harassment. However, the DEOC was recently dissolved.

We understand that noncompliance may be due to existing internal requirements being onerous, redundant, and unnecessary for meeting EEOC requirements. We recommend that DoD evaluate internal requirements to determine which are necessary and can be adhered to, and then come fully into compliance with them.

Recommendations and Timeline for Change

Figure 3.1 describes our recommended timeline for DoD compliance with internal and external directives, as well as combining MEO and

Figure 3.1
Recommended Steps and Timeline for Compliance Initiatives

1.

Ensure 100% Compliance with All EO Directives, Requirements, and Laws

Near Term
Meet all EEOC requirements
Evaluate and modify internal requirements

Medium Term
Issue and implement modified EO requirements
Combine MEO and EEO structures

Long Term
Comply with new Total Force EO
requirements

RAND *RR333-3.1*

EEO organizational structures. In the near term, or the next year, we recommend that DoD come into compliance with current requirements and evaluate existing requirements. Based on the results of this evaluation and with an eye toward the eventual standardization of metrics across services and combining of EO and MEO structures, we also recommend in the near term that DoD create new internal metrics and procedures for evaluating compliance with EO requirements. In the medium term, we recommend that DoD issue and implement these new requirements. In the long term, we recommend that DoD comply with these requirements.

Near Term: 1–12 months
Meet All Equal Employment Opportunity Commission Requirements
We have concerns about the degree to which the military is complying with certain EEOC process requirements, or external requirements. For instance, the EEOC mandates a processing time for employee EO

complaints of 180 days or less; recently, average processing time across DoD has been 288 days (Brown, 2013). There are also some general gaps in compliance with the requirement for federal agencies to submit annual reports to the EEOC: Some federal agencies are not submitting them, and others are submitting but not complying with all of the requirements. This is not a problem specific to DoD (DiversityInc, no date). In the short term, we recommend that DoD come into compliance with external requirements.

Evaluate and Modify Internal Requirements

Earlier in this chapter, we documented noncompliance with internal requirements. We believe that such noncompliance sends a negative message about the degree to which DoD takes seriously its own diversity and inclusion rules. However, it is possible that existing requirements are not being complied with because they are onerous, redundant, or not useful. We recommend evaluating existing requirements to determine to what degree they aid DoD in complying with EO requirements and modifying them in response to findings. In the past, it appears that requirements have been added piecemeal, without a full evaluation of how each new requirement coordinates with or duplicates existing requirements. By evaluating all existing requirements and making holistic judgments, DoD can hopefully come to a more manageable set of requirements that will be sufficient to ensure compliance with internal EO requirements.

Modified requirements should continue to go beyond reporting the demographic makeup of employees. When possible, requirements should include analyses of eligible populations, applicants, selections, and hires, as well as similar analyses regarding promotions. Barrier analysis should be used to determine whether processes can be modified to promote diversity without reducing efficacy. DoD should pay attention to the organizational climate, analyzing issues, such as the prevalence of sexual harassment, that may lead to hostile work environments and/or contribute to higher attrition rates for certain demographic groups, such as women. Another possible topic of interest is racial differences in disciplinary measures. A 1980s study found that black service members were overrepresented among court-martial convictions (Walker, 1992):

it is not clear whether this is still the case, but this could be the sort of metric that DoD would look at as it goes beyond a focus on diversity numbers and looks at the broader environment.

Additionally, at this stage it is important for the services to coordinate to standardize metrics. For instance, we believe that the services have different procedures for collecting race/ethnicity information from service members. While we do not recommend combining EO enforcement across services, we do stress the importance for DoD EO compliance of being able to compare metrics across services.

Medium Term: 1–3 Years
Issue and Implement Modified Equal Opportunity Requirements

In the medium term, we recommend releasing and implementing modified EO and MEO requirements. These should eliminate any existing redundancies and standardize metrics across services and, when possible, across the Total Force, including both military and civilian employees.

Combine Military Equal Opportunity and Equal Employment Opportunity Structures

Additionally, we recommend combining MEO and EEO data-gathering and enforcement structures within each service across the Total Force. For decades, EEO and MEO have processed EO complaints separately. EEO utilizes federally controlled complaint mechanisms, and cases can be judged in a district court if needed. Military cases, on the other hand, are adjudicated through Inspector General, commander-directed investigations, or the chain of command, according to directives. There has been movement on behalf of the Air Force to combine offices to handle both military and civilian EO claims and issues in recent years ("Equal Opportunity Programs Merge Within Air Force," 2008). It is suggested that this merger was designed primarily to save on resources (American Federation of Government Employees Council 214, 2008). Given that DoD is currently staffing two different offices and addressing two parallel sets of procedures, a merger would seem to eliminate some of these duplicative supports. However, there is currently no evidence on how merging civilian and military EO processes would impact cost and effectiveness.

Long Term: 4+ Years
Come in to Compliance with New Total Force Equal Opportunity Requirements

In the long term, DoD should come into compliance with new Total Force EO requirements. Because these requirements are the product of previous stages of evaluation and modification, they should be more effective and DoD should more easily be able to comply with them than with current requirements.

Summary

As DoD expands its diversity goals, it must continue to comply with legal requirements concerning EO, which are similar to requirements at other large organizations, particularly other federal agencies. In addition, it should comply with internal EO requirements, which are best seen as mechanisms for meeting EO mandates rather than as totally separate requirements. After evaluating existing internal requirements, it should modify them to increase efficacy and eliminate redundancy, as well as standardize metrics across services and, when possible, across the Total Force. We also recommend combining EO and MEO functions within each service and, in the long term, coming into compliance with these new requirements.

CHAPTER FOUR

Communication

One major piece of the framework for DoD's new diversity and inclusion policy is improving both internal and external communication. Internal communication can get the DoD workforce on the same page as the leadership in terms of the meaning and importance of diversity and inclusion, as well as provide the workforce with the tools to better manage diversity in service of mission effectiveness. The external piece consists of communicating both with outside stakeholders, such as Congress, regarding diversity efforts and with potential military recruits and civilian employees in order to improve recruiting. The MLDC made several recommendations about the need for strategic communication, both internally and externally:

- **MLDC Recommendation 2:** Leadership training at all levels shall include education in diversity dynamics and training in practices for leading diverse groups effectively.
- **MLDC Recommendation 4:** DoD and the services should inculcate into their organizational cultures a broader understanding of the various types of diversity by using strategic communications plans to communicate their diversity vision and values.
- **MLDC Recommendation 7:** DoD and the services should engage in activities to improve recruiting from the currently available pool of qualified candidates by creating, implementing, and evaluating a strategic plan for outreach to, and recruiting from, untapped locations and underrepresented groups (MLDC, 2011f, p. 29).

In this chapter, we describe the role that communication can play in DoD's new diversity and inclusion efforts. This involves evaluating and modifying both current EO training and current diversity outreach efforts and creating and implementing diversity leadership training. The framework we suggest for this consists of three phases: the short, medium, and long term.

The Importance of Strategic Communication

New initiatives to better recruit and manage a diverse workforce are a priority for DoD leaders, and the MLDC has described communication and initiatives related to communication as a major piece of that. The MLDC defines diversity management as "managing how human differences affect organizational capability, whether differences refer to demographics, cognitive types and skills, place in the organizational structure, or identity within the broader global community" (MLDC, 2011d). Communication can play a large role in this. The DoD Diversity and Inclusion Strategic Plan recommends that to sustain diversity and make leaders accountable, DoD leaders should develop an "authentic, consistent, visible commitment to diversity through strategic communications messaging that resonates" (DoD, 2012a, p. 5). This recommendation emphasizes that the communication must be strategic communication, meaning it must be closely tied to the strategic objectives for diversity. We focus on three reasons for strategic communication as a key component of a successful accountability system to drive change in the area of diversity.

Ensuring Understanding Across the Workforce

One piece of the communication strategy is communicating the new diversity strategy to the DoD workforce. Management literature suggests that leaders of organizations often assume that personnel understand the vision and goals of the organization as well as staff requirements to advance the vision, without enacting a focused communications strategy to ensure this is indeed the case (Gillis, 2011). Personnel cannot be expected to participate in a vision if they do not understand what changes will be taking place, why changes are being made, how changes will affect them, and how they can help to move changes forward. We recommend communicating the new diversity vision to the workforce in a way that is consistent with current organizational values, such as commitment to mission fulfillment.

Research suggests that an existing workforce may be particularly suspicious about any policy that "calls out" differences among them. Care must be taken to communicate the broad diversity vision not just in terms of quotas or EO, but as a way to increase mission effectiveness and to improve organizational outcomes, such as lowered costs, greater creativity, and, particular to DoD, "enhanced efficiency and readiness" (MLDC, 2010b).

Attracting a Diverse Workforce

While strategic communication plays an important role in bringing the existing workforce on board with the new vision of diversity, communication is also important in attracting a diverse group of people to join the DoD workforce. Recruitment plays a critical role in supporting the ability of DoD to meet its mission needs, as well as to meet DoD objectives for having a workforce that is representative of the country. The MLDC (2011b) found that to improve recruitment, a new set of strategies should be developed, many of them focusing on outreach. One example is strategically targeting outreach to underrepresented groups and untapped locations. For instance, many minority college students attend schools that are not Historically Black Colleges and Universities and do not have Reserve Officers Training Corps (ROTC) detachments. In addition, communicating the new vision of diversity, with its focus on leveraging diversity for mission effectiveness, may help to attract a more diverse set of recruits by reassuring these individuals that their differences will not be a barrier to advancement.

Three Principles for Strategic Communication

Strategic communication efforts involve a range of activities, including informing audiences in the short term by managing and distributing information, influencing through long-term persuasion campaigns to "affect attitudinal change," and engaging audiences by building relationships. We draw on guides from the U.S. Joint Forces Command and the U.S. Army, RAND reports, and business literature to describe three principles for increasing the likelihood that strategic communication achieves its desired results.

Strategic Communication Is an Active Process

DoD refers to strategic communication as a "process" (Joint Publication 1-02, 2007). One expert suggests that describing the whole-of-the-enterprise as a process is too vague to be useful, and "the community would be better served by specifying [the process part] as strategic communication planning, integration, and synchronization processes" that "constitute a discrete set of activities and require distinct organization, procedures, and personnel" (Paul, 2010, pp. 11–12). Under this model of strategic communication, leadership goals and objectives are the "inputs" and dissemination products are the ultimate "outputs." We illustrate this process in Figure 4.1. In addition to ensuring that there is planning in the initial stages, successful communication to internal and external audiences "requires diligent and continual analysis and assessment feeding back into planning and action" (U.S. Joint Forces Command, 2009, p. A-3). This suggests that stakeholders must continually assess and adjust communication needs as DoD moves toward its new vision of diversity.

Strategic Communication Is Leadership-Driven but Organizationally Practiced

Effective communication requires "shared responsibility," and strategic communication should be seen to represent the voice of leaders (Paul, 2011). According to DoD documentation, leaders "must decisively engage and drive the strategic communication process. Desired objectives and outcomes are then closely tied to major lines of operation outlined in the organization, command or joint campaign plan" (U.S. Joint Forces Command, 2009). In the private sector, it has been shown that companies that are most effective begin with "clear vision on the intents and purposes . . . with sponsorship from the top" (Merrell and

Figure 4.1
The Strategic Communication Process

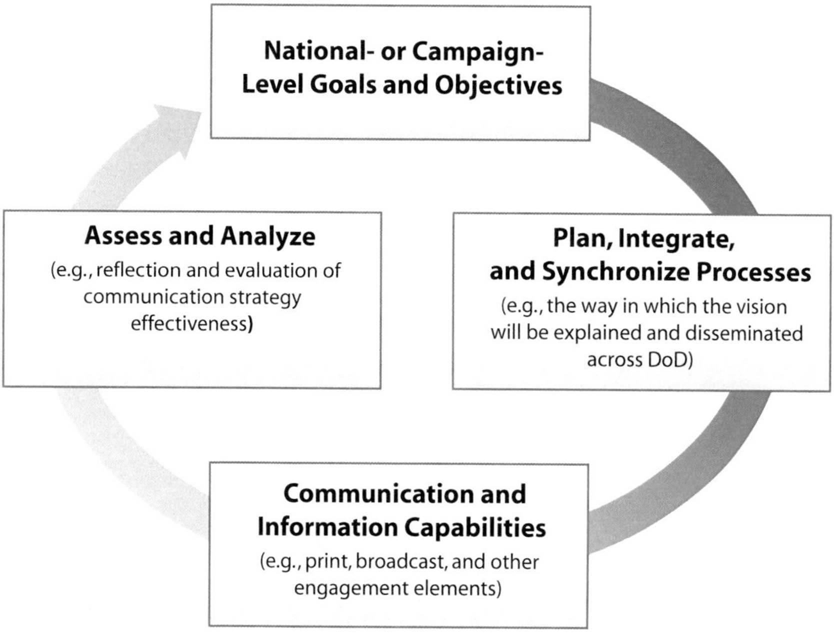

SOURCE: Adapted from Paul, 2011.
RAND *RR333-4.1*

Watson, 2012, p. 20).[1] Strategic communication requires leadership to be central in developing the goals and objectives. Because organizations are complicated and consist of many interrelated moving parts, practicing strategic communication must be an enterprise-wide pursuit. As stated by U.S. Joint Forces Command (2009), "personnel, offices, and mediums must be unified to produce singular, straightforward messages" to achieve optimal effect.

Strategic Communication Is Audience-Attentive

According to the literature, strategic communication is considered strategic in part because of its ability to speak to and inform various audi-

---

[1]   See also Awamleh and Gardner, 1999.

ences. DoD states this simply: "right audience, right message, right time, and right place. . . . Communication strategy must reach intended audiences through a customized message that is relevant to those audiences" (DoD, 2008). Reaching intended audiences requires a concerted effort, and developing a strategic communication plan means conducting formative research in terms of the audience to be reached. How to formulate a message should be built on knowledge of the organization's goals and the population to be reached. To be effective and maintain credibility, messages must be created with an understanding of an audiences' "attitudes, cultures, identities, behavior, history, perspectives and social systems" because "what we say, do, or show, may not be what others hear or see" (Paul, 2011). Although verbal communication will be necessary, other supportive forms, such as posters, ads, policies, and new processes, can be utilized. For example, studies suggest that the generation of Americans born after 1981 is more tech-savvy than previous generations (Bingham and Conner, 2010). New mediums should be considered to communicate with them, as recommended by the DoD Diversity and Inclusion Strategic Plan, which specifically identified the use of social media as important in communicating messages to internal and external audiences.

Recommendations and Timeline for Change

The previous sections provide guidance on why strategic communication is important and what general principles should guide the communication strategy. In this section, we provide recommendations for short, medium, and long-term actions that DoD can take to improve the communication piece of its new diversity and inclusion strategy. This framework is summarized in Figure 4.2.

Figure 4.2
Recommended Steps and Timeline for Communication Initiatives

Educate Current and Future Leaders, Reach Out to Communities

Near Term
Consolidate EO professional training
Develop diversity leadership training
Direct outreach activities to maximize efficiency
Develop clear diversity messages for external audiences

Medium Term
Implement Total Force EO professional training
Implement diversity leadership training
Evaluate return on investment from outreach efforts

Long Term
Develop and implement diversity leadership
    training for all members
Maintain robust outreach efforts

RAND *RR333-4.2*

Near Term: 1–12 Months
Consolidate EO Professional Training

In the short term, we recommend devising consolidated EO professional training. The MLDC's review of DoD training programs suggests that each of the services have different EO training curricula and methods, while EO for the federal agencies appears more consistent. Surveys and informational meetings conducted by the MLDC with service members from the Army, Air Force, Navy, Marine Corps, and Coast Guard reveal that this inconsistency resulted in a mixed "level of awareness and understanding of Service diversity policies" (MLDC, 2011b). Standardization in training materials can help get a consistent message to everyone, enforcing intra-agency unity. Individual services and civilian offices may need to make subtle changes in the presentation of material to support and speak to cultural differences among them. For example, OPM has basic guidelines for diversity training to assist agency managers in designing and delivering programs that promote the inclusion of all personnel to improve mission effectiveness, yet the opportunities for flexibility are also reflected in OPM's training guidelines (U.S. Office of Personnel Management, 2012).

Develop Diversity Leadership Training

In the short term, we recommend that DoD develop new diversity leadership training. The MLDC calls for training in diversity leadership, which is distinct from traditional diversity and EO training. In EO training, individuals focus on "being sensitive to cultural and gender differences" (MLDC, 2011c). Diversity leadership training, on the other hand, shows leaders how to recognize differences and build capabilities, identify new opportunities, and solve problems with them (MLDC, 2011f). Separating diversity training from traditional EO training and integrating it into other leadership training can play an important role in separating the two concepts and ensuring that diversity is seen as equivalent to the many other resources that good leaders must learn to manage and leverage.

According to the MLDC, diversity leadership training should focus on how human differences affect interactions between people and utilize these differences to improve mission effectiveness. Diversity leadership shifts the focus of diversity from counting individuals to the functioning of the unit. It requires leaders to assess the skills of the team members and maximize the ways in which they work together to defeat their opponents. Leaders communicate the value of diversity to subordinates by leading in this way.

The U.S. Army's official field manual, *Army Leadership: Competent, Confident, and Agile* (FM 6-22), provides some guidance on how to lead diverse workgroups: "A leader's job is not to make everyone the same; it is to take advantage of the different capabilities and talents brought to the team. The biggest challenge is to put each member in the right place to build the best possible team" (U.S. Army, 2006, p. 6-3). A new diversity leadership program and training materials can be constructed from existing expertise in the services about leadership training, integrating what is known about diversity leadership training in the literature and among subject-matter experts.

Direct Outreach Activities to Maximize Efficiency

We recommend modifying outreach activities to increase diversity within the DoD workforce. The MLDC made a variety of recommendations along these lines, including developing common applications for ROTC and the service academies, revisiting the admissions processes for the academy preparatory schools, exploring recruiting from two-year colleges, and making recruiters more accountable for minority representation (MLDC, 2011f).

Develop Clear Diversity Messages for External Audiences

We recommend that DoD develop clear messages about its diversity efforts for external audiences. These messages should include the DoD definition of diversity, its diversity goals, and how it is attempting to reach those goals. The messages should be clear and succinct. One major audience for these messages is Congress, which has expressed significant interest in the issue of diversity within the military but may not have up-to-date and accessible information available about DoD diversity work.

Medium Term: 1–3 Years

Implement Total Force Equal Opportunity Professional Training

In the medium term, we recommend that DoD implement the Total Force EO training that was created in the first stage. This will mean consolidating EO training across the services, while preserving some service- and component-specific aspects.

Implement Diversity Leadership Training

We recommend that DoD implement the diversity leadership training that was created in the first stage. This will be an ongoing process, since there are many different leadership training programs within the services, both for enlisted and commissioned service members and for DoD civilians.

Evaluate Outreach Efforts

After modifying DoD diversity recruitment efforts, it will be important to evaluate these to determine which are more successful at reaching DoD goals and modify programs on the basis of the results.

Long Term: 4+ Years
Develop and Implement Diversity Leadership Training for All Members
In the long term, we recommend that DoD implement diversity leadership training for all members, including service members in enlisted and officer training courses, such as the service academies.

Maintain Robust Outreach Efforts
In the long term, we recommend continuing outreach efforts in order to pursue DoD goals of having a diverse workforce based on earlier (and ongoing) assessments of which outreach efforts are the most effective for increasing diversity.

Summary

The second pillar in our framework, communication, plays an important role in supporting the accountability system and driving change by (1) ensuring that all stakeholders understand the vision and how it will be implemented; (2) addressing any issues that may arise as the workforce moves toward are more diverse workforce; and (3) helping to attract a diverse workforce to drive the desired change. However, the communication must be strategic, meaning planned and coordinated in pursuit of a clear set of goals. Strategic communication on diversity should be an active process, with DoD developing a plan around its goals, implementing the plan, evaluating the effectiveness of the communication strategies, and adjusting as necessary. In addition, communication driven by leadership and attentive to the audiences will improve the likelihood of success in meeting DoD goals.

DoD faces a particular challenge in distinguishing between EO policies and the new vision of diversity. One way of doing this is to re-envision diversity training as a key element of traditional leadership training, as opposed to focusing primarily on sensitivity training or informational EO sessions. By communicating through training that the ability to leverage diversity is equivalent to any other leadership quality, the focus should shift from "in groups" and "out groups" to the unique capabilities of all individuals and the impact these capabilities have on mission effectiveness. Communication strategies can also be used to reach external audiences, helping to both ensure DoD's ability to recruit a diverse workforce and ensure that other external stakeholders, such as Congress, understand DoD's diversity activities and the motivation behind them.

CHAPTER FIVE

Coordination

Because responsibility for personnel issues affecting diversity is both dispersed and mostly contained within offices without diversity-specific missions, coordinating efforts across DoD is an important piece of carrying out DoD's new diversity initiatives. Coordinating the many DoD offices tasked with EO and diversity—as well as other ones making personnel decisions affecting diversity—can help lead to improved regulatory adherence across the board, as well as more generally promote DoD's vision of diversity and inclusion. Coordination can also support accountability by improving transparency through standardized monitoring mechanisms (such as metrics for recruiting, promotion, and response time to EO complaints) throughout the organization. Coordination of efforts can save money and time by reducing redundancy.

In this chapter, we summarize the business management literature on the need for coordination and the efforts of DoD to coordinate in developing accountability systems for EO and diversity. We then discuss a few areas of focus that DoD might want to consider in pursuing additional efforts at coordination.

The Importance of Coordination

Management literature suggests that the most effective organizations are those that are goal-directed, and that the commitment of personnel to the organizational goal is essential for success (Li and Hambrick, 2005). Given the complex composition and processes of most organizations, however, it can be difficult to ensure that all parts of an organization are committed to or are working optimally toward the goal (Polzer, Minton, and Swann, 2002). Coordinating various components across the organization can impact planning, management, communication, and effectiveness. This interplay of expertise can allow organizations to facilitate change and face complex issues with renewed innovation and at a faster pace than those organizations that work according to an assembly line model. Further, collaborative coordination can build enthusiasm for change and consolidate resources—both human and financial (Gray, 1989; Schein, 2004). A GAO (2005c, p. 3) study on interagency collaborations suggests that differences in government organizational structures, planning processes, and funding sources have resulted in "a patchwork of programs that can waste scarce funds, confuse and frustrate program customers, and limit the overall effectiveness" of the effort. This is consistent with our general impression of current diversity policy within DoD.

Management literature has cited a number of difficulties in leading an interagency effort, including the lack of a common framework between partners, unclear authority and uncertain power relationships, incompatible ways of communicating, and different organizational core values (Kantor, 1989). A lack of trust can affect coordination as well (Gode-Sanchez, 2010; Jennings and Ewalt, 1998). In recent years, efforts between DoD and the Veterans Administration to coordinate health care revealed that different resources might hinder efforts as well, as "incompatible computer systems . . . inconsistent reimbursement and budgeting policies, and burdensome agreement approval processes" hindered initial health resource–sharing efforts (GAO, 2005c, p. 10).

Prior Coordination Efforts

The 2011 MLDC review of diversity-related policies and programs across DoD suggests that until recent years, the services were independently developing their own diversity definitions, strategies, and programs. In 2005, the Defense Diversity Working Group (DDWG) was developed to synchronize "the efforts of the Services to establish common diversity goals and procedures" (MLDC, 2009b, p. 1). DDWG was first made up of the diversity directors of each service, but has since "expanded to include the Services and Agencies Military Equal Opportunity and Equal Employment Opportunity Directors as well" (Cantor, 2011). Bringing these various leaders together has been helpful in coordinating DoD diversity efforts. DDWG assisted in the creation of new diversity offices within the services and developed the concept and plans for the ODMEO-RAND diversity summit in 2007. However, DDWG is organized at the O-6 or GS-15 level, and we believe this limits its influence: we recommend reorganizing it at a higher level as the Senior Defense Diversity Working Group (SDDWG).

A review of DoD's diversity policies, analysis of its historical and current processes, and discussions with leaders across DoD suggest that further interagency coordination is possible. ODMEO was developed by the Office of Deputy Under Secretary for Equal Opportunity (DUSD[EO]). One of ODMEO's primary goals was and is to ensure that diversity is prioritized in DoD workplace programs and initiatives. MLDC research explains how the organization's realignment both aids and hinders diversity in the total DoD workforce:

> DUSD(EO) was established in 2003, when the Deputy Assistant Secretary of Defense for Equal Opportunity was elevated to the position of DUSD(EO) and the position was filled by a political appointee. When that political appointee departed in 2006, the office of the DUSD(EO) was renamed ODMEO and placed under the DUSD (Plans). On one hand, this realignment mainstreamed diversity and EO by integrating responsibility for these functions into the established organization responsible for "developing and implementing change in high priority areas within . . . Personnel and Readiness" (USD(P&R), 2006). On the other hand, this change dealt two blows: demotion in status and loss of a political appointee position to set and carry out the agenda (Haughton, 2010). When diversity management was added to ODMEO's functions, one existing position was realigned as diversity manager, but no new positions were created (Love, 2010). In 2010,

the position of DUSD (Plans) was eliminated, and ODMEO was placed under the DUSD (Readiness).

Yet a review of ODMEO's diversity portfolio suggests there has been little progress made in some of its key diversity initiatives. Further, "ODMEO remains an understaffed office several levels below the Secretary" (MLDC, 2011d, p. 17). We understand that ODMEO will never be bigger or more powerful than agencies such as the CPP and MPP: It will always have to play an analytic and ombudsman role rather than actually setting personnel policy. For instance, according to DoD Comptroller reports, DoD spent $631.1 million on advertising for Total Force recruiting in 2012 (Office of the Under Secretary of Defense [Comptroller]/Chief Financial Officer, 2012), which is significantly larger than the ODMEO budget. However, by better coordinating with those agencies and by being able to access data that are relevant to diversity and inclusion issues, ODMEO can better inform and influence policies that affect diversity and inclusion within DoD.

Considerations for Enhancing Coordination

While DoD has made significant progress in establishing offices and procedures to ensure coordination, there remain many areas where coordination could be improved. Here we describe several areas in which DoD might consider focusing efforts. In the next section, on recommendations for change, we give more specific ideas.

Leadership Support

Given the complexity of coordinating efforts across a large organization such as DoD, committed leadership is a critical aspect of interagency collaboration. For interagency collaboration, "leadership must set the direction, pace, and tone and provide a clear, consistent rationale that brings everyone together behind a single mission" (GAO, 2003, p. 9). Leaders of coordinated efforts can help their partners prioritize and schedule promoted initiatives as well as delegate authority, adopt policy to different contexts, and negotiate joint benchmarks and measurements. From a higher level, a leader of each organizational effort can recognize the effect that structures and processes have on different efforts, and help devise processes and tools to move agendas forward despite differences (Huxham and Vangent, 2000). Further, accountability to a chief executive in any hierarchy is more easily facilitated if there is an implicit understanding regarding the chain of command (Davies et al., 2010).

Diversity Management

With regard to managing the new accountability system, best organizational management practices suggest that the current configuration is not optimal. Instead, the MLDC recommends creating a position for a chief diversity officer (CDO). A DoD CDO, like a private-sector CDO, would be able to "ensure the sustained emphasis on diversity that has been lacking in the past" (MLDC, 2011d, p. 18). Many business and academic institutions have already developed such an office to coordinate and facilitate diversity efforts. Some CDO duties include the oversight of affirmative action and EEO programs, but when diversity is broadly defined and the relevancy of diversity is included in mission effectiveness, the CDO has a broader portfolio of responsibilities. These include becoming "change management specialists" and agents of change, pointing leaders to issues of diversity, and serving as integration experts in complex institutions (Williams and Wade-Golden, 2007). The MLDC recommends that the CDO report directly to the Secretary of Defense and be responsible for working with the services to standardize data collection and reporting for diversity-related metrics, as well as monitoring EO compliance (MLDC, 2011d). CDOs are leaders in diversity leadership as well, knowing how to harness the capabilities of the workforce to improve the competence and effectiveness of the organization. Their potential duties include maintaining expertise in capability building, helping other leaders develop cross-cultural sensitivity, and learning leadership practices, such as role modeling and communicating (Riche and Kraus, 2009.)

Data Management

Data systems are critical to accountability in that they allow leaders to assess adherence to policies and procedures and ensure the organization is meeting goals for key outcomes of interest. DoD's existing office-specific processes and policies often result in data that are difficult or time-consuming to coordinate in a useful way for acquiring a picture of workforce diversity at any given time. Because of this, a considerable amount of data currently exists that would help DoD get a better picture of diversity and inclusion, but these data are not easily accessible in a useful form to agencies working on diversity policy or personnel policy more generally. It may therefore be useful for DoD to consider establishing a single data repository to consolidate all diversity-related data (MLDC, 2011f).

One Navy tool that may serve as a model is the Navy Military Equal Opportunity Network (MEONet). The system collects information to track progress in resolving formal and informal military EO complaints. Demographic information can be used to analyze internal military EO in the Navy, and summaries of activities and trends are reported to higher Navy headquarters offices, DoD, and other U.S. government agencies (DEOMI, 2010). Another tool is the Bureau of Navy Personnel online system or "BOL," which provides access to active component, enlisted personnel retention statistics—updated monthly—to Navy personnel managers and unit commanders. The data can inform the Navy's actions to improve diversity, including tailored outreach and support services to naval personnel and families. Across DoD, such a tool could generate accurate and timely personnel data that are consistent across the services and that will assist with legal compliance and internal staffing. However, more important than having tools that make accessing data easy is having protocols for data collection that are standardized across time and across services so that the data reported are accurate and comparable.

Issue Focus

As DoD moves toward the new vision for diversity, there are likely to be times when leadership would like to ensure coordinated focus on a single issue. For example, there has been interest in the decision to rescind the exemption of women from direct combat, and the impact it will have on the role of women in Army and Marine Corps units infantry and special operations units. A related issue is the changing physical fitness requirements for women in the Marine Corps, which are increasing the difficulty of the upper body strength component of their physical fitness test for women: Women will, like men, have to do a minimum of three pull-ups, although the rest of the scoring system will still differ for men and women (Bumiller, 2013). To address these special areas of concern, SDDWG can look at trends across the organization, particularly in areas of uncertainty or conflict that may hinder movement toward diversity. By identifying this area as a "hot spot," SDDWG can ensure coordination in the focus of efforts on these special issues of concern. With SDDWG at the helm of organizing efforts, the chances for duplicated efforts and funding will be greatly reduced.

Recommendations and Timeline for Change

The framework, which consists of short-, medium-, and long-term actions, is described in Figure 5.1.

Near Term: 1–12 Months
Organize Senior OSD Taskforce
In the short term, we recommend that DoD organize a senior Office of the Secretary of Defense (OSD) task force with representatives from the various agencies that have responsibility for diversity specifically and personnel policy more generally. At minimum, the task force should include top leaders from ODMEO, MPP, CPP, and the Office of General Council. This will give these top leaders an opportunity to coordinate on policies including outreach, recruiting, training, assignments, promotion, and retention in order to promote greater diversity and a more inclusive work environment. ODMEO has both a small budget and a limited sphere of authority, and so working with the agencies that determine personnel policy is necessary to assuring coordination on policies affecting diversity and inclusion.

Figure 5.1
Recommended Steps and Timeline for Coordination Initiatives

3.

Coordination

Coordinate Diversity Management Efforts for Maximum Efficiency

Near Term
Organize senior OSD task force
(ODMEO, MPP, CPP, Office of General Counsel)
Organize joint senior-only DDWG
Organize special-issue organizations

Medium Term
Create centralized diversity management
system (DDMS)

Long Term
Sustain centralized DDMS

RAND *RR333-5.1*

Organize Joint Senior-Only SDDWG

Currently, the DDWG is established at the O-6 or GS-15 level. We recommend raising it to the general office and Senior Executive Service level. Senior leadership will be able to have more impact on bringing diversity knowledge back to their offices and be effective advocates for DoD's diversity and inclusion vision. We recommend reorganizing it at a higher level as the SDDWG.

Organize Special-Issue Organizations

In the short term, we recommend that DoD organize all organizations that aim to address special issues that are related to diversity and inclusion, which we call "hot spots." The most prominent special-issue organization in recent time is the Sexual Assault Prevention and Response Office (SAPRO), which is responsible for the oversight of DoD sexual assault policy. We contend that sexual assault remains a barrier to DoD creating an inclusive environment for women. SAPRO's efforts represent much of DoD's efforts to prevent and respond to sexual assaults. SAPRO's long-term success depends on the effectiveness of DoD diversity organizations in their effort to ensuring diversity and inclusion as a core value of DoD.

Examples of other "hot spot" issues that can be considered related to diversity and inclusion include the effects of changing personnel policy for women, including lifting of restrictions against women serving in certain military occupations; any emerging impact of the repeal of "Don't Ask, Don't Tell"; and the changing of the Marine Corps physical fitness test to bring the female upper body strength component more in line with the male component. If DoD leaders adopt a more expansive vision of diversity and inclusion, there may be other special-issue organizations that can be included in this new organization. Grouping together special-issue organizations that are synergistic will benefit DoD in several ways. The new organization will make it easier for DoD top leaders to monitor and improve efficiency and effectiveness of these special-issue organizations. More importantly, the new organization will allow DoD senior leaders to demonstrate DoD's commitment to diversity and inclusion to internal and external stakeholders. It will be easier to communicate to the stakeholders about the effort of one coherent organization than the efforts of a collection of quasi-independent special-issue organizations. Most importantly, the membership of the new organization reinforces the scope and underlying meaning of DoD's diversity and inclusion strategic vision.

Medium Term: 1–3 Years
Create a Centralized Diversity Management System

The DoD Diversity Management System (DDMS) would be one way to continue the formal coordination among key stakeholders from both DoD diversity and DoD personnel policy groups. In the medium term, we recommend creating the DDMS structure shown in Figure 5.2. Underneath the top-level structure would be the three divisions created in the short term—the OSD Senior Task Force, the Joint SDDWG, and special-issue groups.

Figure 5.2
**An Example of Formal Coordination Structure: The Defense Diversity
Management System**

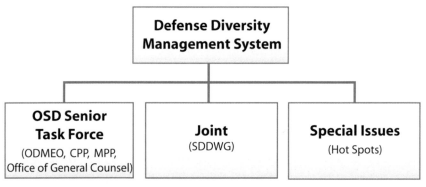

RAND *RR333-5.2*

Long Term: 4+ Years
Sustain Centralized Diversity Management System
In the long term, we recommend sustaining the DDMS. This will keep ensuring that there is a high-level organization with the resources available to advocate effectively for DoD's diversity and inclusion policy throughout the department.

Summary

The U.S. military is one of the largest organizations in the world, so coordination plays a critical role in ensuring that all its components are working simultaneously toward common goals. Accountability systems benefit from transparency and consistency, and coordination can help to overcome a range of barriers that DoD is likely to face in moving toward any major change. DoD has taken steps to improve coordination around diversity, developing the DDWG to help the services synchronize efforts and creating ODMEO under the Office of the Secretary of Defense to oversee uniformity in diversity policy and implementation. However, additional efforts toward coordination are likely to be necessary to realize new goals for diversity. We identify several areas in which coordination could potentially be enhanced to support diversity efforts, including increased leadership support, a specific leadership position for diversity, streamlined data management, and a process to coordinate focus on key diversity issues.

CHAPTER SIX

Conclusion

The framework described in this report offers DoD a way to categorize and prioritize the initiatives in the DoD Diversity Strategic plan published in 2012 and to support DoD's vision and strategies for diversity through an accountability system. We offer the framework as a mechanism for motivating and managing change as well as focusing human and financial resources to reshape the diversity of the total workforce for the long term. ODMEO recognizes the need for an accountability system to guide the planning and implementation of diversity policy and is in the process of designing an accountability framework to guide the development of this system (ODMEO, 2013). We identified three critical components of a framework of change through accountability: complete *compliance* with existent legal codes and DoD policies; strategic *communication* of the vision, goals, and expectations; and thorough *coordination* of effort across the whole organization. By focusing on the three pillars and taking a strategic approach to planning and implementing diversity policy, DoD will be in a better position to succeed in developing and sustaining a strong and diverse workforce.

DoD is likely to face many challenges as it moves toward its new vision for diversity, as it can be difficult to bring system-wide change in an organization that is one of the biggest and most structurally diverse in the world and characterized by frequent turnover in leadership. To conclude this report, we provide two recommendations for DoD as it moves toward developing this new accountability system.

Recommendation 1: Develop the accountability structure for diversity and inclusion based on the framework we proposed.

The framework we proposed is consistent with the *Department of Defense Diversity and Inclusion Strategic Plan, 2012–2017.* Table 6.1 displays how the three Cs can be mapped onto DoD's diversity strategic goals, objectives, actions, and initiatives, specified in the strategic plan.

The compliance pillar of this report correlates with the DoD Diversity and Inclusion Strategic Plan's goal to "develop and update policies and procedures to ensure diversity and inclusion is an institutional priority" (DoD, 2012a, p. 6). This calls for DoD leaders to issue guidance on diversity and institute diversity management policies ensuring merit-based decisions. It also mandates that DoD continue to assess and modify its own diversity policies. This is in service of the larger goal of ensuring leadership commitment to an accountable and sustained diversity effort.

The metrics for the compliance pillar conform to the DoD diversity goal of establishing and implementing a system of accountability reviews. The initiatives consist of identifying key diversity and inclusion indicators, such as career fields and assignments, which lead dis-

Table 6.1
The Three Cs Correlate with DoD Strategic Goals, Objectives, Actions, and Initiatives

Three Pillars	DoD Diversity Strategic Goals	Metrics
Comply	Action 1.1.1	Action 1.1.2 (2nd, 3rd, 4th initiatives)
Communicate		
Internal (Educate)	Action 3.1.1, Action 3.3.1	
External (Awareness)	Objective 2.1, Objective 2.2, Action 1.2.1	
Coordinate	Action 1.1.2 (1st initiative)	

NOTE: Remaining strategic actions concentrate on force sustainment.

proportionately to senior ranks; developing the capability to monitor the scope and impact of DoD diversity efforts; and conducting barrier and trend analysis on key military and civilian diversity indicators to provide guidance to leaders in making informed diversity decisions.

The education piece of the communication pillar corresponds to two actions from the DoD diversity strategic plan: infusing diversity and inclusion throughout both the initial training and socialization process and in leadership training, and reviewing training and development programs to ensure that they draw from all segments of the workforce and identify barriers. Adding diversity and inclusion into socialization and training includes identifying and integrating diversity principles, practices, and competencies; developing a framework to oversee and monitor this; and including diversity and inclusion competencies in leadership assessment. The initiatives to ensure that training and development programs draw from the whole workforce include analyzing the applicant pool and selection data to ensure both full access to development programs and that senior leaders are informed about development and training selections process.

The awareness piece of the communications pillar corresponds to two DoD strategic goals: performing outreach to and recruiting from all segments of society and ensuring that policies and programs support DoD efforts to recruit from a diverse talent pool. To achieve these goals, the strategic plan calls for making sure that recruitment practices are reaching all segments of society, synchronizing outreach and recruitment across DoD, and expanding relationships with stakeholders from institutions including "diverse colleges and universities, trade schools, apprentice programs, Science, Technology, Engineering, and Mathematics (STEM) initiative programs, and affinity organizations" (DoD, 2012a, p. 8).

The coordination piece corresponds to DoD's directive to create a forum of senior leaders to oversee and monitor the diversity and inclusion. The strategic plan situates this initiative as part of improving accountability for diversity outcomes in order to make leadership more committed to diversity and inclusion and accountable for those outcomes. It is also important to communicate to employees that these initiatives, and the larger focus on diversity and inclusion, are a permanent change and not a function of the current political leadership (Terriff, 2007).

Important to note is that many government accountability programs are created "after the fact" of unsatisfactory efforts to reach goals or address problems (Curristine, 2005; Camm and Stecher, 2010). Thus we recommend that DoD begin earlier rather than later. We recommend that initial efforts related to each of the three Cs begin early enough to seed a culture of change through accountability across DoD. A workforce that has accountability ingrained within its culture is more likely to be committed to the diversity vision, no matter who is leading the organization at a given time. By staying focused on accountability, DoD will be able to readily assess its workforce diversity as needed, disclose its performance, and refine and improve the functioning of the system across all components of the organization.

Recommendation 2: Establish a clear timeline of implementation milestones and publish annual status of progress toward these milestones for greatest transparency and accountability for progress.

Accountability must start with DoD diversity organizations, including ODMEO, for the timely implementation of the strategic initiatives. Establishing a clear timeline of implementation milestones will facilitate discussions about resources and responsibilities among the stakeholders whose coordination is essential for successful implementation of the *Department of Defense Diversity and Inclusion Strategic Plan, 2012–2017.*

ODMEO should publish an annual status report on the progress to inform external and internal stakeholders. This annual publication can become an important impetus that sustains the DoD diversity accountability system.

Bibliography

Air Force Policy Directive 36-70, *Personnel Diversity*, Washington, D.C.: U.S. Air Force, October 13, 2010.

Alexander, Ruth, "Which Is the World's Biggest Employer?" *BBC News*, March 19, 2012. As of July 19, 2013:
http://www.bbc.co.uk/news/magazine-17429786

American Federation of Government Employees Council 214, "Memorandum of Agreement on Equal Employment Opportunity (EE)/Military Equal Opportunity (MEO) Merger," June 25, 2008. As of July 23, 2013:
http://afgecouncil214.org/moa/4096/
eeo-equal-employment-opportunity-meo-military-equal-opportunity-merger

Asch, Beth J., Trey Miller, and Alessandro Malchiodi, *A New Look at Gender and Minority Differences in Officer Career Progression in the Military*, Santa Monica, Calif.: RAND Corporation, TR-1159-OSD, 2012. As of July 19, 2013:
http://http://www.rand.org/pubs/technical_reports/TR1159

Awamleh, R., and W. L. Gardner, "Perceptions of Leader Charisma and Effectiveness: The Effects of Vision Content, Delivery, and Organizational Performance," *The Leadership Quarterly*, Vol. 10, No. 3, 1999, pp. 345–373.

Babcock, Pamela, "Diversity Accountability Requires More Than Numbers," *Society for Human Resource Management*, April 13, 2009. As of July 19, 2013:
http://www.shrm.org/hrdisciplines/Diversity/Articles/Pages/MoreThanNumbers.aspx

Bezrukova, K., K. A. Jehn, and C. S. Spell, "Reviewing Diversity Training: Where We Have Been and Where We Should Go," *Academy of Management Learning and Education*, Vol. 11, No. 2, 2012, pp. 207–227.

Bingham, Tony, and Marcia Conner, *The New Social Learning: A Guide to Transforming Organizations Through Social Media*, San Francisco, Calif.: Berrett-Koehler, 2010.

Boudreau, J. W., and P. M. Ramstad, "Human Resource Metrics: Can Measures Be Strategic?" Ithaca, N.Y.: Cornell University, School of Industrial and Labor Relations, Center for Advanced Human Resource Studies, CAHRS Working Paper #98-10, 1998.

Brown, Christopher, "State of IRD Report," Defense Civilian Personnel Advisory Service, 2013.

Bumiller, Elisabeth, "First Pull-Ups, Then Combat, Marines Say," *New York Times*, February 1, 2013. As of July 25, 2013:
http://www.nytimes.com/2013/02/02/us/politics/
first-pull-ups-then-combat-marines-say.html

Camm, Frank, and Brian M. Stecher, *Analyzing the Operation of Performance-Based Accountability Systems for Public Services*, Santa Monica, Calif.: RAND Corporation, TR-853, 2010. As of July 19, 2013:
http://www.rand.org/pubs/technical_reports/TR853

Camp, R. C., *Business Process Benchmarking; Finding and Implementing Best Practices*, Milwaukee, Wisc.: Quality Press, 1995.

Canas, Kathryn, and Harris Sondak, *Opportunities and Challenges of Workplace Diversity* (2nd Edition), Malden, N.J.: Pearson Education, Prentice Hall, 2011.

Cantor, Bradley, "Government-Wide Initiative to Promote Diversity and Inclusion," DoDLive (website), August 25, 2011. As of July 19, 2013:
http://www.dodlive.mil/index.php/2011/08/
government-wide-initiative-to-promote-diversity-and-inclusion

Chief of Naval Personnel Public Affairs, "Diversity in Navy Has New Definition," August 8, 2003. As of July 19, 2013:
http://www.navy.mil/submit/display.asp?story_id=8916

Crystal, David, *English as a Global Language*, Cambridge, England: Cambridge University Press, 2003.

Curristine, Teresa, "Performance and Accountability: Making Government Work," *OECD Observer*, Nos. 252–253, November 2005, pp. 11–12. As of July 19, 2013:
http://www.oecdobserver.org/news/fullstory.php/aid/1697/ Performance_and_accountability:_Making_government_work.html

Davies, P., D. Hill, A. Rudalevige, G. C. Edwards III, J. Virden, and R. Singh, "Prospects for the New U.S. Administration: What Can Social Science Offer?" *European Political Science*, Vol. 9, No. 2, 2010, pp. 244–258.

DeCamp, Jennifer, Sarah O. Meadows, Barry Costa, Kayla M. Williams, John Bornmann, and Mark Overton, *An Assessment of the Ability of the U.S. Department of Defense and the Services to Measure and Track Language and Culture Training and Capabilities Among General Purpose Forces*, Santa Monica, Calif.: RAND Corporation, TR-1192-OSD, 2012. As of July 19, 2013: http://www.rand.org/pubs/technical_reports/TR1192.html

Defense Equal Opportunity Management Institute, United States Navy Military Equal Opportunity Network (MEONet), Version 1.0, 2010. As of July 19, 2013: http://www.deomi.org/EOAdvisorToolkit/documents/MEONETGUIDE2010.pdf

DEOMI—*See* Defense Equal Opportunity Management Institute.

Department of Defense Directive 1350.2, *Department of Defense Military Equal Opportunity (MEO) Program*, Washington, D.C.: U.S. Department of Defense, 1995.

Department of Defense Directive 1440.1, *The DoD Civilian Equal Employment Opportunity (EEO) Program*, Washington, D.C., 1987.

Department of the Navy, *Department of the Navy EEO Program Status Report FY 2010*, 2011, p. 169.

Disney Interactive Media, "About Us: Commitment to Diversity," no date. As of December 2, 2009: http://disney.go.com/disneycareers/dimg/diversity.html

DiversityInc, "No Accountability? 21% of Federal Agencies Don't Submit EEO Reports" no date. As of July 23, 2013: http://www.diversityinc.com/legal-issues/ no-accountability-21-of-federal-agencies-dont-submit-eeo-reports/

DoD—*See* U.S. Department of Defense.

"Equal Opportunity Programs Merge Within Air Force," *Moody Air Force Base News*, May 21, 2008. As of July 19, 2013: http://www.moody.af.mil/news/story.asp?id=123099741

Estrada, A. X., M. C. Stetz, and C. R. Harbke, "Further Examination and Refinement of the Psychometric Properties of the MEOCS with Data from Reserve Component Personnel," *International Journal of Intercultural Relations*, Vol. 31, 2007, pp. 137–161.

Executive Order 13171, *Hispanic Employment in the Federal Government*, October 12, 2000. As of July 23, 2013: http://www.gpo.gov/fdsys/pkg/FR-2000-10-16/pdf/00-26716.pdf

Executive Order 13548, *Increasing Federal Employment of Individuals with Disabilities*, July 26, 2010. As of July 23, 2013: http://www.gpo.gov/fdsys/pkg/FR-2010-07-30/pdf/2010-18988.pdf

Executive Order 13583, *Establishing a Coordinated Government-Wide Initiative to Promote Diversity and Inclusion in the Federal Workforce*, August 18, 2011. As of July 19, 2013:
http://www.whitehouse.gov/the-press-office/2011/08/18/
executive-order-establishing-coordinated-government-wide-initiative-prom

Fernandez, S., and H. G. Rainey, "Managing Successful Organizational Change in the Public Sector," *Public Administration Review*, Vol. 66, No. 2, 2006, pp. 168–176.

GAO—*See* U.S. Government Accountability Office.

General Electric Company, "Our People," no date. As of December 2, 2009:
http://www.ge.com/company/culture/people.html

Gillis, Tamara, *The IABC Handbook of Organizational Communication: A Guide to Communication*, Public Relations, Marketing, and Leadership, San Francisco, Calif.: John Wiley and Sons, 2011.

Gode-Sanchez, Cecile, "Leveraging Coordination in Project-Based Activities: What Can We Learn from Military Teamwork?" *Project Management Journal*, Vol. 41, No. 3, 2010, pp. 69–78.

Gray, Barbara, *Collaboration: Finding Common Ground for Multiparty Problems*, San Francisco, Calif.: Jossey-Bass, 1989.

Haddad, Abigail, Kate Giglio, Kirsten M. Keller, and Nelson Lim, *Increasing Organizational Diversity in 21st-Century Policing: Lessons from the U.S. Military*, Santa Monica, Calif.: RAND Corporation, OP-385, 2012. As of July 23, 2013:
http://www.rand.org/pubs/occasional_papers/OP385.html

Haughton, C., Jr., remarks to the Military Leadership Diversity Commission in Annapolis, Md., March 2010.

Holvino, E., B. M. Ferdman, and D. Merrill-Sands, "Creating and Sustaining Diversity and Inclusion in Organizations: Strategies and Approaches," in M. S. Stockdale and F. J. Crosby, eds., *The Psychology and Management of Workplace Diversity*, Malden, Mass.: Blackwell Publishing, 2004, pp. 245–276.

Hough, L. M., and D. S. Ones, "The Structure, Measurement, Validity, and Use of Personality Variables in Industrial, Work, and Organizational Psychology," in N. Anderson, D. S. Ones, H. K. Sinangil, and C. Viswesvaran, eds., *Handbook of Industrial, Work, and Organizational Psychology. Vol. 1: Personnel Psychology*, London: Sage, 2001, pp. 233–277.

Huxham, C., and S. Vangent, "Leadership in the Shaping and Implementation of Collaboration Agendas: How Things Happen in a (Not Quite) Joined-Up World," *Academy of Management Journal*, Vol. 43, No. 6, 2000, pp. 1159–1175.

Jennings, E. T., and J. G. Ewalt, "Interorganizational Coordination, Administrative Consolidation, and Policy Performance," *Public Administration Review*, Vol. 58, No. 5, September/October 1998, pp. 417–428.

Joint Publication 1-02, *Department of Defense Dictionary of Military and Associated Terms*, Washington, D.C., September 14, 2007.

Kantor, Rosabeth Moss, *When Giants Learn to Dance*, New York: Simon and Schuster, 1989.

Kellermanns, F. W., J. Walter, S. W. Floyd, S. Lechner, and J. C. Shaw, "To Agree or Not To Agree? A Meta-Analytical Review of Strategic Consensus and Organizational Performance," *Journal of Business Research*, Vol. 64, No. 2, 2011, pp. 126–133.

Kirby, Sheila Nataraj, Harry J. Thie, Scott Naftel and Marisa Adelson, *Diversity of Service Academy Entrants and Graduates*, Santa Monica, Calif.: RAND Corporation, 2010. As of November 8, 2013:
http://www.rand.org/pubs/monographs/MG917

Kochan, T., K. Bezrukova, R. Ely, S. Jackson, A. Joshi, K. Jehn, J. Leonard, D. Levine, and D. Thomas, "The Effects of Diversity on Business Performance: Report of the Diversity Research Network," *Human Resource Management*, Vol. 42, No. 1, 2003, pp. 3–21.

Kossek, E. E., and S. C. Zonia, "Assessing Diversity Climate: A Field Study of Reactions to Employer Efforts to Promote Diversity," *Journal of Organizational Behavior*, Vol. 14, 1993, pp. 61–81.

Kraus, A., and M. F. Riche, *Air Force Demographics: From Representation to Diversity*, Alexandria, Va.: CNA, 2006.

Kraus, A., A. K. Hodari, M. F. Riche, and J. Wenger, *The Impact of Diversity on Air Force Mission Performance: Analysis of Deployed Servicemembers' Perceptions of the Diversity/Capability Relationship*, Alexandria, Va.: CNA, 2007.

Li, J., and D. C. Hambrick, "Factional Groups: A New Vantage on Demographic Faultlines, Conflict, and Disintegration in Work Teams," *Academy of Management Journal*, Vol. 48, No. 5, 2005, pp. 794–813.

Lim, Nelson, Michelle Cho, and Kimberly Curry, *Planning for Diversity: Options and Recommendations for DoD Leaders*, Santa Monica, Calif.: RAND Corporation, MG-743-OSD, 2008. As of July 19, 2013:
http://www.rand.org/pubs/monographs/MG743.html

Lim, Nelson, Jefferson P. Marquis, Kimberly Curry Hall, David Schulker, and Xiaohui Zhuo, *Officer Classification and the Future of Diversity Among Senior Military Leaders: Case Study of the Army ROTC*, Santa Monica, Calif.: RAND Corporation, TR-731-OSD, 2009. As of July 19, 2013:
http://www.rand.org/pubs/technical_reports/TR731.html

Lockheed Martin, "Diversity: Forming a New Idea of Diversity," no date. As of May 3, 2013:
http://www.lockheedmartin.com/us/who-we-are/culture.html

Love, J., remarks to the Military Leadership Diversity Commission in Annapolis, Md., March 2010.

Mashaw, Jerry L., "Accountability and Institutional Design: Some Thoughts on the Grammar of Governance," Yale Law School, Public Law Working Paper No. 116, in Michael Dowdle, ed., *Public Accountability: Designs, Dilemmas, and Experiences*, Cambridge. Mass.: Cambridge University Press, 2006, pp. 115–156.

McIntyre, R. M., S. A. Bartle, D. Landis, and M. R. Dansby, "The Effects of Equal Opportunity Fairness Attitudes on Job Satisfaction, Organizational Commitment, and Perceived Work Group Efficacy," *Military Psychology*, Vol. 14, 2002, pp. 299–319.

McMahon, A. M., "Does Workplace Diversity Matter? A Survey of Empirical Studies on Diversity and Firm Performance, 2000–09," *Journal of Diversity Management*, Vol. 5, No. 2, 2010, pp. 37–48.

Melnyk, S., D. M. Stewart, and M. Swink, "Metrics and Performance Measures in Operations Management: Dealing with the Metrics Maze," *Journal of Operations Management*, Vol. 22, 2004, pp. 209–217.

Merrell, P., and T. Watson, "Effective Change Management: The Simple Truth," *Management Services*, Summer 2012, p. 20.

Military Leadership Diversity Commission, *Decision Paper #1, Outreach and Recruiting*, Arlington, Va., 2011a.

———, *Decision Paper #5: Defining Diversity*, Arlington, Va., 2011b.

———, *Decision Paper #6: Diversity Leadership*, Arlington, Va., 2011c.

———, *Decision Paper #7: Implementation and Accountability*, Arlington, Va., 2011d.

———, *Decision Paper #8: Metrics*, January 2011e.

———, *From Representation to Inclusion: Diversity Leadership for the 21st-Century Military*, Arlington, Va., 2011f.

———, *Issue Paper #3, Examples of Diversity Definitions*, Arlington, Va., 2009a.

———, *Issue Paper #7: The Defense Diversity Working Group*, Arlington, Va., 2009b.

———, *Issue Paper #14: Business-Case Arguments for Diversity and Diversity Programs and their Impact in the Workplace*, Arlington, Va., 2010b.

———, *Issue Paper #50, Department of Defense Directive 1020.02: A Foundation for Effective, Accountable Diversity Management? Implementation and Accountability*, Arlington, Va., 2010a.

Millan-Capehart, A., W. L. Grubb, and A. Herdman, "Affirmative Action Decisions: When Ignorance Is Bliss," *Equality, Diversity and Inclusion: An International Journal*, Vol. 28, No. 5, 2009, pp. 415–431.

Milliken, F. J., and L. L. Martins, "Searching for Common Threads: Understanding the Multiple Effects of Diversity in Organizational Groups," *The Academy of Management Review*, Vol. 21, No. 2, 1996, pp. 402–433.

MLDC—*See* Military Leadership Diversity Commission.

Murphy, Dennis, "Talking the Talk: Why Warfighters Don't Understand Information Operations," issue paper for Center for Strategic Leadership, U.S. Army War College, Volume 4-09, May 2009.

National Defense Research Institute, *Sexual Orientation and U.S. Military Personnel Policy: An Update of RAND's 1993 Study*, Santa Monica, Calif.: RAND Corporation, MG-1056-OSD, 2010. As of July 2, 2013: http://www.rand.org/pubs/monographs/MG1056.html

ODMEO—*See* Office of Diversity Management and Equal Opportunity.

Office of Diversity Management and Equal Opportunity, *2012 DoD Diversity and Inclusion Annual Report: Summary Report*, Washington, D.C., 2013.

Office of the Under Secretary of Defense (Comptroller)/Chief Financial Officer, *Operation and Maintenance Overview, Fiscal Year 2013 Budget Estimates*, Washington, D.C., February 2012. As of July 19, 2013: http://comptroller.defense.gov/defbudget/fy2013/fy2013_OM_Overview.pdf

Paul, Christopher, "Strategic Communication Is Vague: Say What You Mean," *Joint Force Quarterly*, No. 56, Quarter 1, 2010, pp. 10–13.

———, *Strategic Communication: Origins, Concepts, and Current Debates*, Santa Barbara, Calif.: Praeger, 2011.

Pfeffer, Jeffery, and Robert I. Sutton, *The Knowing-Doing Gap: How Smart Companies Turn Knowledge into Action*, Cambridge, Mass.: Harvard Business School Press, 2000.

Polzer J. T., L. P. Minton, and W. B. Swann, "Capitalizing on Diversity: Interpersonal Congruence in Small Work Groups," *Administrative Science Quarterly*, Vol. 47, 2002, pp. 296–324.

Public Law 88–352, Civil Rights Act of 1964, Title VII, 42 U.S. Code 2000e, 2009.

Public Law 110-417, Duncan Hunter National Defense Authorization Act for Fiscal Year 2009, October 14, 2008.

Public Law 112-239, National Defense Authorization Act for Fiscal Year 2013, January 02, 2013.

Rapert M. I., A. Velliquette, and J. A. Garretson, "The Strategic Implementation Process: Evoking Strategic Consensus through Communication," *Journal of Business Research*, Vol. 55, No. 4, 2002, pp. 301–310.

Riccucci, N. M., "Cultural Diversity Programs to Prepare for Work Force 2000: What's Gone Wrong?" *Public Personnel Management*, Vol. 26, No. 1, 1997, pp. 35–41.

Richard, O. C., "Racial Diversity, Business Strategy, and Firm Performance: A Resource-Based View," *Academy of Management Journal*, Vol. 34, No. 2, 2000, pp. 164–177.

Riche, Martha Farnsworth, and Amanda Kraus, *Approaches to and Tools for Successful Diversity Management: Results from 360-Degree Diversity Management Case Studies*, Alexandria, Va.: CNA Corporation, CNA Research Memorandum D0020315, 2009.

Riche, Martha Farnsworth, Amanda Kraus, and April K. Hodari, *The Air Force Diversity Climate: Implications for Successful Total Force Integration*, Alexandria, Va.: CNA Corporation, 2007.

Riche, Martha Farnsworth, Amanda Kraus, April K. Hodari, and Jasen P. DePasquale, *Literature Review: Empirical Evidence Supporting the Business-Case Approach to Work Force Diversity*, Alexandria, Va.: CNA Corporation, CNA Research Memorandum D0011482.A2, 2005.

Scheider, B., M. G. Ehrhart, and W. H. Macey, "Organizational Climate and Culture," *Annual Review of Psychology*, Review in Advance, July 30, 2012. As of July 19, 2013:
http://www.annualreviews.org/doi/pdf/10.1146/annurev-psych-113011-143809

Schein, Edgar H., *Organizational Culture and Leadership*, San Francisco, Calif.: Jossey-Bass, 2004.

Scott, T., R. Mannion, H. Davies, and M. Marshall, "The Quantitative Measurement of Organizational Culture in Health Care: A Review of the Available Instruments," *Health Services Research*, Vol. 38, No. 3, 2003, pp. 923–945.

Shaw, B, "Affirmative Action: An Ethical Evaluation," *Journal of Business Ethics*, Vol. 7, 1988, pp. 763–770.

Stavridis, J. G., "Strategic Communication and National Security," *Joint Force Quarterly*, 3rd Quarter, 2007.

Stecher, Brian M., Frank Camm, Cheryl L. Damberg, Laura S. Hamilton, Kathleen J. Mullen, Christopher Nelson, Paul Sorensen, Martin Wachs, Allison Yoh, Gail L. Zellman, with Kristin J. Leuschner, *Toward a Culture of Consequences: Performance-Based Accountability Systems for Public Services*, Santa Monica, Calif.: RAND Corporation, MG-1019, 2010. As of July 19, 2013:
http://www.rand.org/pubs/monographs/MG1019.html

Terriff, Terry, "Of Romans and Dragons: Preparing the US Marine Corps for Future Warfare," *Contemporary Security Policy*, Vol. 28, No. 1, 2007, pp. 143–162.

Thomas, K., *Diversity Dynamics in the Workplace*, Belmont, Calif.: Wadsworth, 2005.

Thompson, Donna E., and Laura E. Gooler, "Capitalizing on the Benefits of Diversity Through Workteams," in E. E. Kossek and S. A. Lobel, eds., *Managing Diversity: Human Resource Strategies for Transforming the Workplace*, Malden, Mass.: Wiley, 1996.

Tilles, E. A., "Lessons from Bakke: The Effect of Grutter on Affirmative Action in Employment," *University of Pennsylvania Journal of Labor & Employment Law*, Vol. 6, No. 2, 2004, pp. 451–465.

Tsui, A. S., and B. A. Gutek, *Demographic Differences in Organizations*, Lanham, Md.: Lexington, 1999.

Tsui, A., T. Egan, and C. O'Reilly, "Being Different: Relational Demography and Organizational Attachment," *Administrative Science Quarterly*, Vol. 37, No. 4, 1992, pp. 549–579.

Under Secretary of Defense, Personnel and Readiness, Memorandum, "Improving Diversity Through Realignment of the Equal Opportunity Office," Washington, D.C.: U.S. Department of Defense, 2006.

U.S. Army, *Army Leadership: Competent, Confident, and Agile*, FM 6-22, Washington, D.C.: Headquarters, Department of the Army, October 26, 2006. As of July 23, 2013:
http://usacac.army.mil/cac2/Repository/Materials/fm6-22.pdf

U.S. Census Bureau, "An Older and More Diverse Nation by Midcentury," press release, August 2008. As of July 19, 2013:
http://www.census.gov/newsroom/releases/archives/population/cb08-123.html

U.S. Department of Defense, *Principles of Strategic Communication*, memorandum from the Principal Deputy Assistant Secretary of Defense for Public Affairs, August 15, 2008. As of July 19, 2013:
http://www.au.af.mil/info-ops/documents/principles_of_sc.pdf

———, *Quadrennial Defense Review Report*, Washington, D.C., 2010.

———, *Department of Defense Strategic Management Plan, FY2012–FY2013*, September 9, 2011. As of July 19, 2013:
http://dcmo.defense.gov/publications/documents/FY12-13%20SMP.pdf

———, *Department of Defense Diversity and Inclusion Strategic Plan, 2012–2017*, Washington, D.C., 2012a. As of July 19, 2013:
http://diversity.defense.gov/Portals/51/Documents/DoD_Diversity_Strategic_Plan_%20final_as%20of%2019%20Apr%2012%5B1%5D.pdf

———, *Sustaining U.S. Global Leadership: Priorities for 21st Century Defense*, January 3, 2012b. As of July 19, 2013:
http://www.defense.gov/news/Defense_Strategic_Guidance.pdf

U.S. Department of Defense, Office of the Assistant Secretary of Defense for Public Affairs, "Defense Department Rescinds Direct Combat Exclusion Rule; Services to Expand Integration of Women into Previously Restricted Occupations and Units," press release, January 24, 2013. As of July 23, 2013:
http://www.defense.gov/releases/release.aspx?releaseid=15784

U.S. Equal Employment Opportunity Commission, *Equal Employment Opportunity Management Directive 715: Federal Responsibilities Under Section 717 of Title VII and Section 501 of the Rehabilitation Act*, October 1, 2003. As of July 23, 2013:
http://www.eeoc.gov/federal/directives/md715.cfm

U.S. Government Accountability Office, *Results-Oriented Cultures: Implementation Steps to Assist Mergers and Organizational Transformations*, Washington, D.C., GAO-03-669, July 2003. As of July 19, 2013:
http://www.gao.gov/assets/240/238749.pdf

———, *Equal Employment Opportunity: The Policy Framework in the Federal Workplace and the Roles of EEOC and OPM*, Washington, D.C., GAO-05-195, 2005a. As of July 19, 2013:
http://www.gao.gov/new.items/d05195.pdf

———, *Military Personnel: Reporting Additional Servicemember Demographics Could Enhance Congressional Oversight*, Washington, D.C., GAO-05-952, 2005b. As of July 23, 2013:
http://www.gao.gov/assets/250/247843.pdf

———, *Results-Oriented Government: Practices That Can Help Enhance and Sustain Collaboration among Federal Agencies*, Washington, D.C., GAO-06-15, October 2005c. As of July 19, 2013:
http://www.gao.gov/new.items/d0615.pdf

———, *Equal Employment Opportunity: Improved Coordination Needed Between EEOC and OPM in Leading Federal Workplace EEO*, Washington, D.C., GAO-06-214, 2006. As of April 25, 2013:
http://www.gao.gov/assets/260/250521.pdf

———, *Federal Chief Information Officers: Opportunities Exist to Improve Role in Information Technology Management*, Washington, D.C., GAO-11-634, 2011. As of July 23, 2013:
http://www.gao.gov/new.items/d11634.pdf

U.S. Joint Forces Command, *Commander's Handbook for Strategic Communication and Communication Strategy*, Joint Warfighting Center, Suffolk, Va., 2009. As of July 19, 2013:
http://www.au.af.mil/au/awc/awcgate/jfcom/cc_handbook_sc_27oct2009.pdf

U.S. Marine Corps, Information for Military Leadership Diversity Commission (MLDC), briefing presented to the Military Leadership Diversity Commission in Washington D.C., April 2010.

U.S. Office of Personnel Management, *Fiscal Year 2010 Federal Equal Opportunity Recruitment Program Report*, Washington, D.C., 2010.

U.S. Office of Personnel Management, "Frequently Asked Questions," web page, no date. As of October 19, 2013:
http://www.opm.gov/diversityandinclusion/faq/index.aspx

———, "Training and Development Policy: Guidelines for Conducting Diversity Training," web page, no date. As of October 15, 2012:
http://www.opm.gov/hrd/lead/policy/divers97.asp

———, *Guidance for Agency-Specific Diversity and Inclusion Strategic Plans*, Washington, D.C., November 2011. As of July 19, 2013:
http://www.opm.gov/diversityandinclusion/reports/
DIAgencySpecificStrategicPlanGuidance.pdf

Voinovich, George V., *Report to the President: The Crisis in Human Capital*, Washington, D.C.: U.S. Senate Subcommittee on Oversight of Government Management, Restructuring, and the District of Columbia of the Senate Committee on Governmental Affairs, 2000. As of July 19, 2013:
http://www.hsgac.senate.gov/download/
report-to-the-president-on-the-crisis-in-human-capital-sen-voinovich

Von Bergen, W. C., B. Soper, and T. Foster, "Unintended Negative Effects of Diversity Management," *Public Personnel Management*, Vol. 31, No. 2, 2002, pp. 235–251.

Walker, Martin R., *An Analysis of Discipline Rates Among Racial/Ethnic Groups in the US Military*, DTIC Document, 1992.

Williams, Damon A., and Katrina Wade-Golden, "The Chief Diversity Officer," *CUPA HR Journal*, Vol. 58, No. 1, Spring and Summer 2007, pp. 38–48.

Williams, Juan, and Julian Bond, *Eyes on the Prize: America's Civil Rights Years, 1954–1965*, New York: Penguin Books, [1988] 2002.

Willoughby, K., and C. O'Reilly, "Demography and Diversity in Organizations: A Review of Forty Years of Research," in B. M. Staw and L. L. Cummings, eds., *Research in Organizational Behavior*, Vol. 20, Greenwich, Conn.: JAI, 1998, pp. 77–140.